D1716285

THE PROPYLAIA TO
THE ATHENIAN AKROPOLIS

VOLUME I

THE PREDECESSORS

THE PROPYLAIA TO
THE ATHENIAN AKROPOLIS

VOLUME I

THE PREDECESSORS

BY

WILLIAM B. DINSMOOR, JR.

THE AMERICAN SCHOOL OF CLASSICAL STUDIES AT ATHENS
PRINCETON, NEW JERSEY
1980

Both the initial research and the publication of this work were made possible in part through grants from the National Endowment for the Humanities, a Federal agency whose mission is to advance knowledge and understanding of the humanities.

Library of Congress Cataloging in Publication Data

Dinsmoor, William B   1923–
    The Propylaia to the Athenian Akropolis.

    CONTENTS: v. 1. The predecessors.
    1. Athens. Propylaea. 2. Athens–Antiquities.
3. Excavations (Archaeology)–Greece, Modern–Athens.
4. Greece, Modern–Antiquities. I. Title
DF287.P75D56   726'.1'20809385   79-9232
ISBN 0-87661-940-5 (v. 1)

PRINTED IN GERMANY *at* J. J. AUGUSTIN, GLÜCKSTADT

TO MY EVER HELPFUL WIFE

ANASTASIA

PREFACE

William B. Dinsmoor began his work on the Propylaia in Athens in 1910. At that time the earlier gateway building, which for convenience will be termed hereafter the Propylon, was to be treated as an extremely minor part of the publication since little new material could be added to that which had already been published in the article of C. Weller in *AJA*, ser. 2, 8, 1904. As a result, my father never exhibited much interest in this part of the study. He did, however, make two important discoveries. The first of these, which came to light in 1910 during his excavation in the north aisle of the Propylaia, was a rock cutting which indicated a wider Propylon than the ones formerly restored by Dörpfeld and Weller; he also envisaged a deeper building than those shown in earlier published restorations, with an inner gate wall over the wide rock cutting which had long been exposed in the central aisle of the Propylaia and where his predecessors had placed the east façade of the structure. His only communications of these findings were his oral ones to J. Bundgaard in 1939 and to G. Stevens (who misinterpreted them) prior to 1942, and his own published ones, in the form of a square outline to indicate the outer limits of the Propylon in plan, on his drawings of the Akropolis in *AJA* 51, 1947, and in *The Architecture of Ancient Greece,* 1950. In the latter publication he made brief mention, on page 198, that the earlier gate building formed a large square, that it probably had four, rather than two, columns *in antis* at each façade, that it had an interior gate wall, and that it made plentiful use of poros (this last is certainly incorrect for the original construction). He never drew any actual restored plan of the building.

His second important discovery occurred in 1918 when he conducted excavations within the Southwest Wing of the Propylaia and discovered additional rock cuttings for the steps of the forecourt, but he never published this information and gave only cursory verbal description of it to Bundgaard and Stevens, neither of whom ever saw the cuttings. At this same time he measured the exposed part of the forecourt as well, and Plates 2, 7, and 8, and Plan A of the following text derive from his sketches and notes. The information for the now buried krepidoma of the Propylon was also supplied through his recordings.

For the text, his compilation of the findings and thoughts of the early investigators of the building, up until 1936, was very helpful, but it has necessarily been altered from the form in which he had envisaged it because of my organization of the subject matter into its various periods. Certain of his beliefs, such as that the "tripod base" supported a Hekataion, and that the flank walls of the Propylon were carried up in mud-brick construction, have been presented in the text as possibilities, but I also include my own alternative interpretation of these installations; where his thoughts of 50 to 67 years ago are completely disproved by later findings, I have unceremoniously altered them.

Since it is now my lot to continue the study of the Propylaia, I naturally began with the early Propylon, about which more has come to light than was known before my father's demise in 1973.

This new information is based in large degree on my own studies of, and discoveries concerning, the building. I have also had to verify and rectify the early annotations of my father and, more important, to bring them up to date over the last 40 years. Because of this work, I have been able to segregate, and to allocate to their various periods in time, the several phases of the entrance to the Akropolis prior to the Mnesiklean Propylaia. The resulting architectural study of each phase is something that had never been attempted before. In past studies, including those of my father in note form, the entire construction was lumped, to all intents and purposes, into one phase, with only vague mention of possible earlier and later periods.

I am most desirous of completing the far-from-finished volume which is concerned with the Mnesiklean Propylaia, on which my father had labored for many years and on which I spent the year 1962/63 making drawings for the text and plates, but an enormous amount of work still remains to be done on it. Rather than delay publication of this volume on the Predecessors of the Propylaia in order to await completion of the entire project, I have decided that this first part of the over-all study should appear now.

I am greatly indebted to my father for that part of the work which he was able to accomplish for the following study of the early Propylon. Had he not initiated this undertaking, I would most likely not have done so nor continued it and carried it to its conclusion.

I wish to thank, at this belated time, the Archaeological Institute of America for the Olivia James Fellowship of 1962/63 which allowed me to measure and draw the Propylaia; although these drawings will not appear until my work on the Mnesiklean building is completed, the opportunity given me at that time to study the structure whetted my appetite for the entire problem of the entrance to the Akropolis in its various phases. I also wish to thank most gratefully the National Endowment for the Humanities which awarded me the grant in 1977 that allowed me to finish this part of the over-all study and also to continue, as far as time permitted, with the manuscript of the Mnesiklean Propylaia.

My warmest appreciation also goes to Drs. N. Platon and G. Dontas, the Ephors of the Akropolis in 1962 and 1977 respectively, for their permission to work on the site.

The American School of Classical Studies at Athens, in the persons of Professors James McCredie and Henry Immerwahr, and the Directors, past and present, of the Excavations of the American School at the Athenian Agora, Professors Homer A. Thompson and T. Leslie Shear, Jr., have been extremely helpful in connection with this present work.

The German Archaeological Institute in Athens has kindly provided me with certain of the photographs for the plates, while the greater body of them were taken by the expert hand of Eugene Vanderpool, Jr.

Lastly, I want to express my appreciation for the cleaning operation conducted and financed by H. Eiteljorg in 1975, under the supervision of John Camp, during which new evidence came to light for the early history of the entrance to the Akropolis.

ATHENS, 1977   WILLIAM B. DINSMOOR, JR.

TABLE OF CONTENTS

LIST OF ILLUSTRATIONS

ABBREVIATIONS AND BIBLIOGRAPHY

AJA = *American Journal of Archaeology*

AEMittOest = *Archaeologisch-Epigraphische Mitteilungen aus Österreich-Ungarn*

AthMitt = *Mitteilungen des deutschen archäologischen Instituts. Athenische Abteilung*

BCH = *Bulletin de correspondance hellénique*

Δελτίον = *Δελτίον Ἀρχαιολογικόν*

Hermes = *Hermes. Zeitschrift für klassische Philologie*

JdI = *Jahrbuch des deutschen archäologischen Instituts*

RevArch = *Revue archéologique*

Adam, S. (1966), *The Technique of Greek Sculpture* (British School of Archaeology at Athens, Supplementary volume 3), London.

Amandry, P. (1976), "Trépieds d'Athènes: I. Dionysies," *BCH* 100, pp. 15-93.

Baumeister, A. (1885-1888), *Denkmäler des klassischen Altertums,* Munich and Leipzig.

Baumgarten, F., Poland, F. and Wagner, R. (1913), *Die hellenische Kultur,* 3rd ed., Leipzig and Berlin.

Beloch, J. (1912-1916), *Griechische Geschichte,* 2nd ed., I-II, Strassburg.

Berve, H. and Gruben, G. (1966), *Greek Temples, Theaters and Shrines,* New York.

Beulé, M. (1853), *L'Acropole d'Athènes* (Lebouteux, draftsman), Paris.

– (1862), *L'Acropole d'Athènes,* 2nd ed., Paris.

– (1868), *Histoire de l'art grec. avant Périclès,* Paris.

Beyer, I. and Preisshofen, F. (1977), "Die Datierung der großen Reliefgiebel des alten Athenatempels der Akropolis," *Archäologischer Anzeiger* [*JdI* 92], pp. 44-84.

Boersma, J. S. (1970), *Athenian Building Policy from 561/0 to 405/4 B.C.,* Groningen.

Bötticher, A. (1888), *Die Akropolis von Athen,* Berlin.

Bohn, R. (1880a), "Bericht über die Ausgrabungen auf der Akropolis zu Athen im Frühjahr 1880, I," *AthMitt* 5, pp. 259-267.

– (1880b), "Zur Basis der Athena Hygieia," *AthMitt* 5, pp. 331-334.

– (1882), *Die Propyläen der Akropolis zu Athen,* Berlin and Stuttgart.

Borrmann, R. (1904), *Die Baukunst des Altertums und des Islam in Mittelalter,* Leipzig.

Broneer, O. (1958), "Excavations at Isthmia, Third Campaign, 1955-1956," *Hesperia* 27, pp. 1-37.

Bundgaard, J. A. (1957), *Mnesicles,* Copenhagen.

– (1974a), "Le sujet de *IG* I² 24," *Mélanges helléniques offerts à Georges Daux,* Paris, pp. 43-49.

– (1974b), *The Excavation of the Athenian Acropolis 1882-1890,* Copenhagen.

– (1976), *Parthenon and the Mycenaean City on the Heights,* Copenhagen.

Burnouf, E. (1850), "Les Propylées," *Archives des missions scientifiques et littéraires,* ser. 1, 1, pp. 8–38.

− (1877), *La ville et l'acropole d'Athènes aux diverses époques,* Paris.

Bury, J. (1900), *A History of Greece to the Death of Alexander the Great,* London.

Buschor, E. (1922), "Burglöwen," *AthMitt* 47, pp. 92–105.

Busolt, G. (1897), *Griechische Geschichte bis zur Schlacht bei Chaeroneia* III, Gotha.

Carpenter, R. (1970), *The Architects of the Parthenon,* Baltimore.

Carroll, M. (1907), *The Attica of Pausanias,* Boston.

Casson, S. (1937), "Note on the Use of the Claw-Chisel," *AJA* 41, pp. 107–108.

Chaudet, M. (1852), "Propylées de l'acropole d'Athènes," *RevArch,* ser. 1, 9, pp. 288–298.

− (1853), "Propylées de l'acropole d'Athènes," *RevArch,* ser. 1, 10, pp. 151–159.

Choisy, A. (1899), *Histoire de l'architecture,* Paris.

Collignon, M. (1910), *Le Parthénon,* Paris.

− (1914), *Le Parthénon,* 2nd ed., Paris.

Coulton, J. J. (1977), *Greek Architects at Work,* London.

Curtius, E. (1891), *Die Stadtgeschichte von Athen,* Berlin.

Daremberg, C. and Saglio, E. (1877–1919), *Dictionnaire des antiquités grecques et romaines,* Paris.

De Sanctis, G. (1912), Ἀτθίς, Turin. (Cf. *Atthis,* Florence *ca.* 1975.)

− (1927), "Cronache e commenti," *Rivista di filologia e d' istruzione classica* 55 (n.s. 5), pp. 557–565.

Dickens, G. (1912), *Catalogue of the Acropolis Museum* I, Cambridge.

Dinsmoor, W. B. (1913), "Studies of the Delphian Treasuries, II. The Four Ionic Treasuries," *BCH* 37, pp. 5–83.

− (1934), "The Date of the Older Parthenon," *AJA* 38, pp. 408–448.

− (1935), "The Older Parthenon: Additional Notes," *AJA* 39, pp. 508–509.

− (1937), "Peisistratos, Kleisthenes, Aristeides, Themistokles oder Kimon? Wer hat den älteren Parthenon begonnen?" *JdI* 52, pp. 3–13.

− (1939a), *The Athenian Archon List in the Light of Recent Discoveries,* New York.

− (1939b), "Archaeology and Astronomy," *Proceedings of the American Philosophical Society* 80, pp. 95–173.

− (1942), "The Correlation of Greek Archaeology with History," *Studies in the History of Culture: The Disciplines of the Humanities* (American Council of Learned Societies), Menasha, Wisconsin, pp. 185–216.

− (1947), "The Hekatompedon on the Athenian Acropolis," *AJA* 51, pp. 109–151.

− (1950), *The Architecture of Ancient Greece,* London.

Dörpfeld, W. (1885), "Der alte Athena-Tempel auf der Akropolis zu Athen," *AthMitt* 10, pp. 275–277.

− (1886a), "Ueber die Ausgrabung auf der Akropolis," *AthMitt* 11, pp. 162–169.

− (1886b), "Der alte Athenatempel auf der Akropolis," *AthMitt* 11, pp. 337–351.

− (1887), "Der alte Athenatempel auf der Akropolis," *AthMitt* 12, pp. 25–61.

− (1891), "Athenatempel auf der Akropolis von Athen," *Antike Denkmaeler* I, p. 1.

− (1892), "Der ältere Parthenon," *AthMitt* 17, pp. 158–189.

− (1897), "Der alte Athena-Tempel auf der Akropolis," *AthMitt* 22, pp. 159–178.

− (1902), "Die Zeit des älteren Parthenon," *AthMitt* 27, pp. 379–416.

− (1911a), "Zu den Bauwerken Athens," *AthMitt* 36, pp. 39–72.

− (1911b), "Gesimse unter Wandmalereien," *AthMitt* 36, pp. 87–96.

− (1929), review of D. S. Robertson, *A Handbook of Greek and Roman Architecture,* Cambridge 1929, *Berliner philologische Wochenschrift* 49, pp. 1244–1250.

− and Reisch, E. (1896), *Das griechische Theater,* Athens.

D'Ooge, M. L. (1908), *The Acropolis of Athens,* New York.

Dyer, T. H. (1873), *Ancient Athens,* London.

Eiteljorg, H. (1975), "New Finds Concerning the Entrance to the Athenian Acropolis," *Athens Annals of Archaeology* 8, pp. 94–95.

Fabricius, E. (1886), "Das platäische Weihgeschenk in Delphi," *JdI* I, pp. 176–191.

Fougères, G. (1911), *Grèce,* Paris.

− (1914), *Athènes,* Paris.

− (n.d.), "Propylum, Propylaeum, Propylaea," in Daremberg and Saglio, IV, pp. 686–690.

Fowler, H. and Wheeler, J. (1909), *A Handbook of Greek Archaeology,* New York.

Frazer, J. G. (1898), *Pausanias's Description of Greece,* London.

Friederichs, C. and Wolters, P. (1885), *Die Gipsabgüsse antiker Bildwerke in historischer Folge erklärt,* Berlin.

Furtwängler, A. (1878), "Die Chariten der Akropolis," *AthMitt* 3, pp. 181–202.

− (1906), *Aegina: das Heiligtum der Aphaia,* Munich.

Gardner, E. (1902), *Ancient Athens,* London.

Gardner, P. (1892), *New Chapters in Greek History,* London.

Gruben, G. (1966), *Die Tempel der Griechen,* Munich.

− (1976), *Die Tempel der Griechen,* 2nd ed., Munich.

− *See also* Berve.

Guhl, E. and Koner, W. (1893), *Leben der Griechen und Römer,* 6th ed., Berlin.

Guillaume, E. (1877), "Acropolis," in Daremberg and Saglio, I, pp. 37–44.

Guillon, P. (1943), *Les trépieds du Ptoion,* Paris.

Gulick, C. (1911), *The Life of the Ancient Greeks,* New York.

Harrison, E. (1965), *The Athenian Agora,* XI, *Archaic and Archaistic Sculpture,* Princeton.

Harrison, J. (1899), "Hecate," in Daremberg and Saglio, III, pp. 45–52.

− (1906), *Primitive Athens,* Cambridge.

− and Verrall, M. (1890), *Mythology and Monuments of Ancient Athens,* London.

Heberdey, R. (1919), *Altattische Porosskulptur,* Vienna.

Hellström, P. (1975), "The Asymmetry of the Pinacotheca − Once More," *Opuscula Atheniensia,* ser. 5, 11, pp. 87–93.

Hill, B. H. (1906), "Notes on the Hekatompedon Inscription (*I.G.* I, *Suppl.* p. 138)," *AJA,* ser. 2, 10, p. 82.

− (1912), "The Older Parthenon," *AJA* 16, pp. 535–558.

Hill, I. T. (1953), *The Ancient City of Athens,* London.

Hitzig, H. and Blümner, H. (1896). *See* Pausanias.

Hodge, A. T. (1975), "Bevelled Joints and the Direction of Laying in Greek Architecture,"
    AJA 79, pp. 333-347.
Hoffer, J. *See* Schöll, A. (1841).

Iakovidis, S. (1962), Ἡ Μυκηναϊκὴ Ἀκρόπολις τῶν Ἀθηνῶν, Athens.

Johannowski, W. (1958), "Atene," in *Enciclopedia dell'arte antica classica e orientale* I, Rome,
    pp. 767-863.
Judeich, W. (1905), *Topographie von Athen* (*Handbuch der Altertumswissenschaft* III.2.2), Mu-
    nich.
— (1929), "Hekatompedon und alter Tempel," *Hermes* 64, pp. 391-415.
— (1931), *Topographie von Athen* (*Handbuch der Altertumswissenschaft* III.2.2), 2nd ed., Munich.

Kavvadias, P. (1889), «Ἀνασκαφαὶ ἐν τῇ Ἀκροπόλει», Δελτίον, pp. 49-50.
— and Kawerau, G. (1906), *Die Ausgrabung der Akropolis vom Jahre 1885 bis zum Jahre 1890,*
    Athens.
Kern, O. (1913), *Inscriptiones Graecae,* Bonn.
Klein, W. (1904), *Geschichte der griechischen Kunst* I, Leipzig.
Köster, A. (1909), *Das Pelargikon,* Strassburg.
Kolbe, W. (1936), "Die Neugestaltung der Akropolis nach den Perserkriegen," *JdI* 51, pp. 1-64.
Kraus, T. (1960), *Hekate, Studien zu Wesen und Bild der Göttin in Kleinasien und Griechenland,*
    Heidelberg.

Leake, W. (1821), *The Topography of Athens,* 1st ed., London.
Lebouteux. In Beulé, M. (1853).
Lechat, H. (1891), "Les sculptures en tuf de l'acropole d'Athènes," *RevArch,* ser. 3, 17, pp. 304-
    333.
— (1904), *La sculpture attique avant Phidias,* Paris.
Lolling, H. (1889), "Hellenische Landeskunde und Topographie," *Geographie und politische
    Geschichte des klassischen Altertums,* Nördlingen, pp. 101-352.
— (1890a), «Ἑκατόμπεδον. Συμβολαὶ εἰς τὴν ἱστορίαν τῶν ἐπὶ τῆς Ἀκροπόλεως ναῶν τῆς Ἀθη-
    νᾶς», Ἀθηνᾶ 2, pp. 627-662.
— (1890b), «Ἐπιγραφαὶ ἐκ τῆς Ἀκροπόλεως», Δελτίον, pp. 92-98.
Luckenbach, H. (1905), *Die Akropolis von Athen,* Munich and Berlin.
Lübke, W. (1899), *Grundriß der Kunstgeschichte* I, 2nd ed., Stuttgart.
Luria, S. (1927), "Zur Geschichte der Präskripte in den attischen voreuklidischen Volksbeschlüs-
    sen," *Hermes* 62, pp. 257-275.

Matton, L. and R. (1963), *Athènes et ses monuments,* Athens.
Michaelis, A. T. F. (1862), "Die Balustrade am Tempel der Athena Nike auf der Akropolis
    von Athen," *Archäologische Zeitung,* pp. 266-267.
— (1876), "Bemerkungen zur Periegese der Akropolis von Athen," *AthMitt* 1, pp. 275-307.
— (1877), "Bemerkungen zur Periegese der Akropolis von Athen," *AthMitt* 2, pp. 85-106.
—, ed. (1901), *Arx Athenarum a Pausania descripta* (O. Jahn, ed.), 3rd ed., Bonn.
—, ed. (1923), *Das Altertum* (A. Springer, *Handbuch der Kunstgeschichte* I), 12th ed., Leipzig.

Middleton, J. H. (1892), *Notebook F,* one of six unpublished notebooks prepared for his un-finished *Topography of Athens,* now in the library of the Fitzwilliam Museum, Cambridge.
- (1900), *Plans and Drawings of Athenian Buildings* (Society for the Promotion of Hellenic Studies, Supplementary paper 3, E. A. Gardner, ed.), London.
Milchhöfer, A. (1885), "Die Akropolis," in Baumeister, pp. 200–209.
Miller, W. (1893), "A History of the Akropolis of Athens," *AJA,* ser. 1, 8, pp. 473–556.

Oliver, J. (1933), "Selected Greek Inscriptions," *Hesperia* 2, pp. 480–513.

Pantelidou, M. (1975), Αἱ Προϊστορικαὶ Ἀθῆναι, Athens.
Paton, J. M., ed. (1927), *The Erechtheum,* Cambridge, Massachusetts.
Pausanias, ι, H. Hitzig and H. Blümner edd., Berlin and Leipzig 1896.
Penrose, F. (1851), *An Investigation of the Principles of Athenian Architecture* (T. J. Willson, architect), London.
- (1888), *An Investigation of the Principles of Athenian Architecture,* 2nd ed., London.
Petersen, E. (1880), "Die dreigestaltige Hekate," *AEMittOest* 4, pp. 140–174.
- (1881), "Die dreigestaltige Hekate (Fortsetzung)," *AEMittOest* 5, pp. 1–84.
- (1908a), *Athen,* Leipzig.
- (1908b), "Nachlese in Athen. II. Artemis-Hekate, Hermes, Chariten," *JdI* 23, pp. 16–32.
Picard, C. (n.d.), *L'Acropole, L'Enceinte – L'Entrée – Le bastion d'Athéna Niké – Les Propylées,* Paris.
Plommer, H. (1960), "The Archaic Akropolis: some Problems," *Journal of Hellenic Studies* 80, pp. 127–159.

Raubitschek, A. (1949), *Dedications from the Athenian Akropolis,* Cambridge, Massachusetts.
Reinach, S. (1888), *Voyage archéologique en Grèce et en Asie Mineure, sous la direction de m. Philippe Le Bas,* Paris.
- (1897), *Répertoire de la statuaire grecque et romaine* II, Paris.
Reisch, E. (1890), *Griechische Weihgeschenke (Abhandlungen des archäologisch-epigraphischen Seminares der Universität Wien* VIII), Vienna.
Robert, C. (1880), "Der Ausgang zur Akropolis," in Klessling, A. and von Wilamowitz-Möllen-dorff, U., *Aus Kydathen,* Berlin, pp. 173–194.
Robertson, D. S. (1945), *A Handbook of Greek and Roman Architecture,* Cambridge.
Ross, L. (1855), *Archäologische Aufsätze* I (E. Schaubert, architect), Leipzig.

Schaubert, E. *See* Ross, L. (1855).
Schede, M. (1922), *Die Burg von Athen,* Berlin.
Schöll, A. (1841), "Ansichten der Akropolis zu Athen und ihrer Gebäude" (J. Hoffer, architect), *Allgemeine Bauzeitung mit Abbildungen für Architekten* (Vienna), pp. 91–125.
Schrader, H. (1905), "Der Cellafries des alten Athenatempels auf der Akropolis," *AthMitt* 30, pp. 305–322.
- (1928), "Die Gorgonenakrotere und die ältesten Tempel der Athena auf der athenischen Akropolis," *JdI* 43, pp. 54–89.
Shear, T. L., Jr. (1970), "The Monument of the Eponymous Heroes in the Athenian Agora," *Hesperia* 39, pp. 145–222.

– (1971), "The Athenian Agora: Excavations of 1970," *Hesperia* 40, pp. 241–279.

Sitte, H. (1910), "Ein attisches Hekataion," *Jahreshefte des österreichischen archäologischen Instituts in Wien* 13, pp. 87–94.

Smith, A. H. (1900), *A Catalogue of Sculpture in the Department of Greek and Roman Antiquities, British Museum* II, London.

Spaulding, L. (1906), "On Dating Early Attic Inscriptions," *AJA,* ser. 2, 10, pp. 394–404.

Stevens, G. (1936), "The Periclean Entrance Court of the Acropolis of Athens," *Hesperia* 5, pp. 443–520.

– (1946), "Architectural Studies concerning the Acropolis of Athens," *Hesperia* 15, pp. 73–106.

Tiberi, C. (1964), *Mnesicle l'architetto dei Propilei,* Rome.

Tomlinson, R. (1976), *Greek Sanctuaries,* London.

Travlos, J. (1960), Πολεοδομικὴ Ἐξέλιξις τῶν Ἀθηνῶν, Athens.

– (1971), *Pictorial Dictionary of Ancient Athens,* London.

Vanderpool, E. (1974), "The Date of the Pre-Persian City-Wall of Athens," Φόρος, *Tribute to B. D. Meritt,* D. W. Bradeen and M. F. McGregor, edd., Locust Valley, New York, pp. 156–160.

Von Rohden, H. (1888), "Propyläen," in Baumeister, pp. 1414–1422.

Walter, O. (1952), "Die Parthenonfundamente und das delphische Orakel," *Anzeiger der österreichischen Akademie der Wissenschaften in Wien* 89, pp. 97–107.

Weickert, C. (1929), *Typen der archaischen Architektur in Griechenland und Kleinasien,* Augsburg.

Weller, C. (1903), "The Pre-Periclean Propylon of the Acropolis at Athens," *AJA,* ser. 2, 7, pp. 93–94.

– (1904), "The Pre-Periclean Propylon of the Acropolis at Athens," *AJA,* ser. 2, 8, pp. 35–70.

– (1913), *Athens and its Monuments,* New York.

Welter, G. (1922), "Das Olympieion in Athen," *AthMitt* 47, pp. 61–71.

– (1923a), "Vom Nikepyrgos," *AthMitt* 48, pp. 190–201.

– (1923b), reported in "Chronique des fouilles," *BCH* 47, pp. 507–508.

Wiegand, T. (1904), *Die archaische Poros-Architektur der Akropolis zu Athen,* Cassel and Leipzig.

Wilhelm, A. (1898), "Altattische Schriftdenkmäler," *AthMitt* 23, pp. 466–492.

Willson, T. J. *See* Penrose, F. (1851).

Winter, F. (1912), "Griechische Kunst," in Gercke, A. and Norden, E., *Einleitung in die Altertumswissenschaft* II, 2nd ed., Leipzig and Berlin, pp. 75–166.

Wolters, P. (1890), "Zum Alter des Niketempels," *Bonner Studien (Aufsätze aus der Altertumswissenschaft Reinhard Kekulé),* Berlin, pp. 92–101.

SYNOPSIS

From the time of the first Mycenaean settlement on the Akropolis, the main entrance must have occupied the western end of the hill, where the approach is the most gentle and accessible. The Mycenaean gateway, however, was totally eradicated by the building of the Archaic Propylon (Pl. 1).[1] Then the Propylon, in turn, as well as the northern part of the Mycenaean fortification wall, was demolished in 437 B.C. to make room for the Propylaia of Mnesikles. Fortunately for us, certain remains of the Propylon and of its forecourt, which did not interfere with the newer building, were allowed to remain.

In past studies, the Propylon and the stepped forecourt have generally been considered as belonging to the same building program. A second phase of the Propylon, one of repair, has occasionally, but vaguely, been mentioned. It will be shown in the following study of the complex that there were actually four distinct periods, and a sub-phase, in the construction of the early 5th-century entrance.

The first of these was of the pre-Propylon period, when the area which lies just outside the southern length of the Pelasgian wall, at the west end of the Akropolis, and immediately south of the Mycenaean entrance to the citadel, was transformed into a theatral area which presumably allowed seating for spectators of the Panathenaic procession and also provided accommodation for the display of dedications (Pls. 2, 3). The form which this area took was that of an L, or actually a stunted Z, consisting of a combination of cut bedrock and built-up poros steps (ABCD, Pl. 2). The top step supported a series of marble benches and also, it would appear, a number of bases for dedications which were backed up with a marble dado of metopes re-used from the Archaic Hekatompedon. Presumably this rock-cut forecourt extended northwards to the very early gate. Its date of construction must have been about 489–488 B.C.

Within a very few years, prior to 480 B.C. and the sack of Athens by the Persians, work on the marble Propylon was started, with a more easterly axis than had the earlier gate. First were erected the front steps and stylobate, which were cut neatly to fit against the pre-existing rock-cut steps and the metope lining of the Pelasgian wall, almost as if their sole function was to create a change of level from west to east (Pl. 4:B). The diverging line of metopes, extending into the area of what was to become the Propylon, was most certainly still standing, since the two slabs at the southern terminus of the stylobate were respected by the later construction. Then, again within this same decade, further work on the project was undertaken. The northern extension of the Pelasgian wall, beyond the present anta wall of the Propylon, was now removed, along with its lining of marble slabs, and the northernmost of these metopes extant today was trimmed down to the level of the

---

[1] In further discussion of the gate buildings, the Archaic one will be referred to solely as the Propylon, to differentiate it from the Classical successor, the Propylaia of Mnesikles.

stylobate. The temporary hiatus in the building construction was perhaps caused by arguments of the military leadership against the dismantlement of this massive wall.[2] Now, also, the side walls of the Propylon were built with their great marble orthostates and underlying, projecting platform courses (Pl. 4:C). Within the building, the bedrock was cut down into horizontal planes, at different levels as dictated by the natural configuration of the surface, in order to present a solid bearing for the interior stair and for the floor slabs and their underpinning. The finished floor of this period, however, was probably never installed. The erection of antae near the ends of the façades, and presumably of four intervening columns as well, had certainly been started, since the protective surface on top of the stylobate was removed to create a bed surface for the southwest anta, but it is doubtful that the structure was completed prior to 480 B.C., when its orthostates and projecting platform blocks sustained fire damage from the Persian attack.

The final phase of the Propylon was that of its extensive rebuilding after the war, probably in the 460's under Kimon. The projecting platform under the interior orthostates was crudely reworked. Its upper course was dressed back to the line of the orthostates of the wall, and its lower one was transformed into a low bench. The interior was now paved with a makeshift flooring. An anta wall of poros blocks and a marble anta, of smaller dimensions than the original one, were installed on the stylobate at the southwest corner of the building, and presumably at the other three corners as well (Pl. 4:D). Much of the reconstruction beyond this point is conjectural, since the evidence is missing, but the gate house was presumably rebuilt in some fashion before it was almost totally demolished to make way for the Propylaia of 437 B.C. The last work done on the Propylon of which we have any evidence is the hacking down of the western bench block along the southern wall, next to the anta wall. At this time a dedication of some sort, which had been resting on top of the bench, was moved down into a socket cut into the new floor space.

---

[2] In later years Mnesikles was not allowed to disturb the southern part of this same wall for his Southwest Wing.

I

THE PREHISTORIC ENTRANCE AND THE LITERARY SOURCES

The form and exact location of the entrance to the Mycenaean Akropolis is somewhat conjectural.[1] That there was a gateway at the west end of the hill is indisputable, since this is the side with the most gentle approach and was therefore the one which was also used for the main entrance from the Archaic period onwards. The early gate must have pierced a now missing link of the Pelasgian circuit wall which ran perpendicular to the extant part of the wall on the west end of the Akropolis. The physical evidence, however, is lacking both for the gate and for the wall that enclosed it on its western side.

Among the earliest attempts at a restoration of that part of the Pelasgian wall which faced the western approach were those of Michaelis in 1901 (Pl. 5)[2] and Köster in 1909.[3] The former merely indicated the beginning of the missing northern continuation, perpendicular to and completing the enframing of the Archaic Propylon at its northwest corner; no suggestion was made as to the disposition of the Mycenaean gateway. The latter, completely disregarding the Propylon, continued the extant portion of the Mycenaean wall in a straight line towards the northeast, and did not show a main gateway. Of the more recent and comprehensive studies, that of Stevens in 1946[4] took into consideration, for the first time, certain archaeological evidence: a small section of curving wall in the forecourt of the later Propylaia and the corner of what is purportedly a prehistoric house beneath the Pinakotheke.[5] He took the present northern limit of the Pelasgian wall, at the southwest corner of the Propylon, as being the original limit,[6] and projected perpendicularly from it his restored gate wall; he proceeded to loop this early wall around to the north and then to the east, to incorporate the extant curved portion of wall in front of the Propylaia and to contain the remnant of the prehistoric "house" beneath the Pinakotheke (Pl. 1). He thereby created a defensible court, before the gate, between his restored wall and the Mycenaean *pyrgos* (which lies under the Athena Nike bastion). This restoration, with the addition of a theoretical second, outer gate, which varies in location according to the source, also formed the basis of the later plans of Travlos and Iakovidis in 1960, 1962, 1971, and 1975 (Pl. 1).[7]

[1] The most comprehensive study of this subject is by Spyridon Iakovidis, Ἡ Μυκηναϊκὴ Ἀκρόπολις τῶν Ἀθηνῶν.

[2] Michaelis, 1901, pl. XVII.

[3] Köster, 1909, fig. IV:b.

[4] Stevens, 1946, pp. 73–77.

[5] Kavvadias and Kawerau, 1906, pl. Β΄. Cf. Bundgaard, 1974b, pl. 1.

[6] This is now known to be impossible in that cuttings in the bedrock show a northern continuation, from this point, of the marble metopes which lined the wall in the early 480's, proving that the wall itself continued further north.

[7] Travlos, 1960, fig. 7, and 1971, fig. 67; also in Pantelidou, 1975, p. 31. Iakovidis, 1962, dwgs. 34, 35, 38.

1

The major problem with these restorations is that they do not properly take into consideration
the logical relationship of the later, Archaic Propylon to the earlier walls. Immediately prior to the
construction of the gatehouse of the 480's, part of the Pelasgian wall, including the Mycenaean
gate, was necessarily demolished. For the Propylon to act also as a gate, it needed walls on either
side of it, and it must have been fitted into the gap which was created for it. We have the evidence
of this at the southwest corner of the building where the ragged, awkward juncture it formed with
the pre-existing wall still remains. Logic, which often provides the only answer to certain problems, tells us that the northwest corner of the Propylon was most probably similarly connected to
the missing, northern continuation of the Pelasgian wall. This likelihood was recognized by
Michaelis in 1901 (Pl. 5). Stevens, in 1946, was unable to connect the earlier and later constructions because of the conditions he imposed for the course of the Mycenaean wall, and so he
restored a new fortification wall at the time of the Propylon, partly overlying the earlier one and
partly tracing a new route of its own, to tie in with the northwest corner of the Archaic gatehouse
(Pl. 5).[8] Travlos, in 1960, connected his western-lying Pelasgian wall to the Propylon with a short,
makeshift cross wall;[9] by 1971, he accepted an earlier idea that apsidal Building B had previously
occupied the area of the Pinakotheke,[10] and he placed this Archaic structure on top of the Pelasgian wall, which he thus obliterated before the time of the Propylon at the crucial juncture, doing
away entirely with the problem (Pl. 1).[11]

Although Stevens' restoration of the route of the Pelasgian wall seems at first glance to make
sense (if considered without reference to the Archaic Propylon), further study of it casts doubts
on its credibility. The small segment of curving wall which still exists to the west of the Propylaia,
and which forms an essential component of his scheme, is built of comparatively small stones
which are most dissimilar in character to the large boulders that compose the still extant parts of
the Pelasgian wall. As Bundgaard stated:[12] "I cannot agree that they formed part of a fortress wall
of the same type as the Pelasgian wall. They are too small to come from the façade, and lie so close
to a drop in the surface of the rock that there is no room for façade blocks beyond them." They
much more likely formed part of a retaining wall for a terrace outside the fortifications.[13] As for the
corner of a prehistoric "house" beneath the Pinakotheke, which Stevens felt ought to be enclosed
within the walls, its possible location either within or without the fortifications is purely conjectural. The Akropolis was inhabited by the ruler and his entourage, while the Mycenaean city occupied the south and north slopes and probably the area to the west of the hill as well.[14] The argument that this structure, with its relatively thin walls of 0.50 m. and less, should have been within

---

[8] Stevens, 1946, pp. 75, 78.

[9] Travlos, 1960, p. 35.

[10] Shown by Bundgaard, 1957, fig. 40, as lying outside the Pelasgian wall. See Dörpfeld, 1911a, p. 54, and Heberdey, 1919,
p. 178. Strong evidence against the belief that apsidal Building B once occupied the site of the Pinakotheke, however, comes from
the very same foundation wall, between the Pinakotheke and the Northeast Hall of the Mnesiklean structure, which has previously
been used as evidence for such a location of Building B. Bundgaard (1976, p. 39) states that this foundation consists exclusively of
stones from Buildings B and I. The southern half of this wall, which was first erected, is formed from carefully aligned re-used wall
blocks. It is only the northern half, which Mnesikles erected after a hiatus during the construction of this part of the Propylaia, which
contains the elements of the entablature of two Archaic structures, one of them being Building B. Since Building B, if it had been
located beneath the Pinakotheke, would have interfered with the new construction, it would have been dismantled at an early stage
by Mnesikles. Conversely, if it had existed here and been dismantled at an early stage, one would expect the elements from the
upper entablature to have been the first members to be used in the adjacent foundation of the Pinakotheke. Such is not the case
here.

[11] Travlos, 1971, fig. 71.

[12] Bundgaard, 1957, note 62.

[13] The walls are generally dated to the 13th century B.C., which was the period of the great Mycenaean fortifications. Prior to
this, the Mycenaean sites seem not to have been so heavily defended. It is possible that this terrace, and the *pyrgos* to the south, date
to an earlier period, but were retained after the great walls were built.

[14] Pantelidou, 1975, pp. 251–257.

the fortification is weak, especially since one cannot be sure that it is Mycenaean or even that it was a house; the two extant walls are not at right angles and the outer corner, if one ever existed, is broken away. Furthermore, the theory has presented another problem. In order to thread the Pelasgian wall tortuously through the narrow gap between the "house" wall and the western limit of the foundations of the Pinakotheke (it is generally agreed that the evidence precludes a still greater western encroachment of the fortification wall), this restored wall becomes quite thin when compared to those of Mycenae and Tiryns, to the other extant remains on the Athenian Akropolis, and especially to its own companion section just to the south, which is almost 6 meters in width.

Aside from a problem that the twisting Pelasgian wall, as shown by Iakovidis and Travlos (Pl. 1), drastically limits the "house" in size, it is unbelievable, based on the very fact that part of this relatively fragile "house" still exists, that some of the massive Pelasgian wall would not also be preserved under the protective cover of the later Pinakotheke. There would have been no reason to remove the Mycenaean wall, and yet not a trace is preserved in this area. Since, moreover, the wall of Stevens' looping scheme cannot be tied into the northwest corner of the later Propylon, I feel that it is best to put aside his restoration, along with those of Iakovidis and Travlos, and to look for a happier solution.

If we turn for a moment to Mycenae and Tiryns, we note that the entrance areas to both citadels are rectangular. The fortified forecourt in front of the gate at Mycenae is *ca.* 7.25 m. wide, while the similarly serving fortified corridor at Tiryns is somewhat narrower. One might expect a comparable arrangement at Athens (Iakovidis' court is less than 4 meters wide, while that of Travlos, although almost 8 meters in width, is quite confining in the other direction, less than 11 meters, with the result that the space is about that of a good-sized living room). If, as seems to be a requirement for the setting of the Propylon, the northern run of the Pelasgian wall tied in at the northwest corner of that Archaic gate building, and if this wall ran just to the east of north, more or less parallel with the extant southern stretch, there would be a clear width of about 10 meters for a fortified court between the walls (Pl. 1, my restoration).

The logical general routing of the missing Pelasgian wall was shown by Dinsmoor in 1947,[15] and was basically accepted and followed by Bundgaard in 1957,[16] although, with the latter's more northerly orientation of the northern extension of the wall, thereby placing a considerable mass of it within the confines of the Pinakotheke, one would expect, as with the Stevens scheme, that some traces of the construction would have remained in this protected area. The solution given first by Dinsmoor in 1947 meets the problem more sensibly than do other published schemes and has been accepted here with modifications. The northern extension of the west wall has been angled slightly in my study to avoid completely that part of the Pinakotheke which has been cleared and which shows no traces of the wall, and yet not angled so greatly that the Archaic cistern at the northwest corner of the Akropolis could not be included within its limits, since the wall and cistern certainly co-existed at one time. Also, as mentioned earlier, this same wall has been continued south of the northwest corner of the later, Archaic Propylon in order to create a defensible forecourt in front of the Mycenaean gate, which has been restored with the same width as that employed for the Lion Gate at Mycenae (Pl. 1). As for the original continuation of this northern wall to the south of the northwest corner of the Propylon, the physical evidence is certainly no less than it is for the earlier restorations of Stevens, etc. To the north, the Roman

[15] Dinsmoor, 1947, p. 122, fig. 3.
[16] Bundgaard, 1957, figs. 34, 40, and 1976, pl. K:1.

cistern in the Northeast Hall of the Propylaia destroyed any traces of earlier remains. We cannot, of course, know the exact orientation of the northern run of wall, nor the point of its southern termination, nor the exact location of the Mycenaean gate (which must have been closer to the one shown by Bundgaard than to those shown by Stevens, Iakovidis, and Travlos).[17] Although my restoration, like the earlier ones, is somewhat conjectural, I feel, however, that it has the advantage of possessing a more authentic Mycenaean appearance than do those published before.

The entrance of the 13th century B.C. must have continued in use, with possible modifications, down into the 5th century B.C. The earliest recorded event during which this gateway is mentioned took place in the reign of Peisistratos, when he assumed the tyranny for the third time, in 546 B.C. The story was related by Aristotle in the *Athenian Constitution,* 15 (transl. Sandys):

> (Peisistratus, returning from Eretria, had defeated the Athenians in the battle of Pallene, and entered the city.) He then deprived the people of their arms in the following manner. Having organized an armed muster in the Theseum, he began to harangue the troops in a feeble voice, and, on their saying that they could not hear him plainly, he then urged them to move up the hill to the Propylon of the Acropolis, in order that he might make himself better heard. While he thus wasted time with rhetorical speech, those appointed to this work carried off the arms and shut them up in the houses near the Theseum; then they returned to Peisistratus and gave him a signal. Whereupon he, terminating his speech on other matters, spoke about the arms, saying that it was not an occurrence which should surprise them or cause them to lose heart, but that it was their duty to return to their private business, while he would take charge of all public affairs.

The same story was repeated by Polyainos in his work on *Stratagems in War* (I. 21. 2) except that he uses the term *propylaion.* We thus have evidence that a structure called the Propylon or Propylaion existed at this early a date. Its form, however, probably differed very little from that of the Mycenaean entrance.

Another incident, but one which is to be associated with the entrance in the Archaic period, was that of its burning by the Persians in September, 480 B.C. The story is given to us by Herodotos, VIII. 51-53 (transl. Godley):

> (The Persians) took the city, then left desolate; but they found in the temple some few Athenians, temple-stewards and needy men, who defended themselves against the assault by fencing the acropolis with doors and logs . . . (and) by rolling great stones down on the foreigners when they assaulted the gates; insomuch that for a long while Xerxes could not take the place, and knew not what to do. But at last in their quandary the foreigners found an entrance . . . . In front of the acropolis, and behind the gates and the ascent thereto, there was a place where none was on guard and none would have thought that any man would ascend that way; here certain men mounted near the shrine of Cecrops' daughter Aglaurus, though the way led up a sheer cliff . . . . Those Persians who had come up first betook themselves to the gates, which they opened, and slew the suppliants; and when they had laid all the Athenians low, they plundered the temple and burnt the whole of the acropolis.

---

[17] Bundgaard shows an original, northern continuation from the extant southern wall of *ca.* 13.5 m. prior to the gate wall (Bundgaard, 1957, p. 45, fig. 34).

It might possibly be objected that this narrative fails to mention the Propylon so definitely as to make the identification certain; but the only alternative, the gates of the lower Pelargikon,[18] seems to be exluded because the Persians were apparently within ("behind") these gates, and also because the rolling stones suggest the steeper slope below the Propylon itself.

It has been suggested that Herodotos (v. 77) twice again alluded to a Propylon, in speaking of the Chalkidian fetters and quadriga which were set up on the Akropolis after the Athenian victory of 506 B.C. Here we find the two terms *megaron* and *propylaia* (transl. Godley with slight revisions):

> The fetters in which the prisoners had been bound they hung up in the acropolis; these were preserved in my time, hanging from walls that the Medes' fire had charred, opposite the megaron facing west. Moreover, they dedicated a tenth part of the ransoms, having made of it a four-horse chariot; this stands first on the left on entering the propylaia in the acropolis . . . .

Of these it is most likely that the megaron was the west end of the Peisistratid temple of Athena. The Propylaia in question were probably the Propylon, but the wall on which the fetters hung was certainly not part of that building as was proposed by Ross (see below, footnote 25, p. 43). We may conclude, therefore, that the only ancient allusions to early gate buildings are those of Aristotle and Polyainos with reference to the stratagem of Peisistratos in 546 B.C., and those of Herodotos in connection with the Chalkidian quadriga and with the gates of the Akropolis in 480 B.C. The first must be concerned with a late form of the Mycenaean gate, and the second with the Propylon itself.

Not only these literary passages, but also the configuration of the ascent, gave Leake, in 1821, reason to suppose that a pre-Periklean gateway had existed, even though remains of such a gateway were not yet visible at his time.[19]

---

[18] Weller (1904, p. 66, note 1) prefers to identify the gates as belonging to "the Pelargicon wall lower down. The order of the words τῶν πυλέων καὶ τῆς ἀνόδου seem to indicate this. Furthermore, the Propylon, like the Propylaea, was not meant, and could not have served, as a work of defense; nor is it thinkable that the defenders would have allowed their assailants to approach so near the summit before offering resistance." Köster was of the same opinion (1909, pp. 26–27). The theory that Herodotos referred to the Propylon, however, was held by Ross (1855, p. 81), Fougères (1911, p. 27; n.d., p. 688), and Schede (1922, p. 49).

[19] Leake, 1821, p. 189; cf. Ross, 1855, p. 81, note.

II
MODERN INVESTIGATIONS OF THE PROPYLON

E xcavations undertaken on eight occasions, in 1840, 1880, 1889, 1901, 1910, 1918, 1946, and 1975, brought to light the remains of a structure which, because of its location, may without question be identified as a Propylon, and, because of its relative level and partial removal, must certainly be dated earlier than the Mnesiklean Propylaia. Yet the surviving remains are so insignificant that the restorations of the missing portions, and the theories as to date, are very diverse. The more important excavations were followed by detailed studies of the building, published by Ross, Bohn, and Weller. Numerous independent investigators have made detailed observations of great value. It will be our first task to array the evidence gathered by our predecessors in this field.

1840–1880

Actual traces of the Propylon were first discovered during the excavations by Pittakis in 1840.[1] These remains formed three groups, taken in order from south to north: (I) two lines of steps meeting almost at a right angle, of which one side is backed against the Pelasgian wall (here faced with marble slabs) south of the Southwest Wing of the Mnesiklean Propylaia; (II) a marble stylobate supporting a marble anta and a poros anta wall, forming an obtuse angle with the Pelasgian wall, together with an inner side wall faced with marble, at right angles to the anta wall, all in the corner between the Southwest Wing and the Central Building of the Propylaia; and (III) cuttings in the bedrock under the great central doorway of the Propylaia (Pl. 6).[2] These traces were only partially cleared by Pittakis, so that the earliest descriptions are incomplete. No report was published with regard to the excavations themselves; we learn from a statement by Schöll merely that the triangle which was formed between the poros parastas (anta wall) and the side wall, in area II, was filled with an ancient deposit of clay utensils, bronze, and mussel shells.[3]

The official study of the remains is that written by Ross in 1841, but not published until 1855.[4] As a result of this delay in publication, the remains were incompletely and incorrectly interpreted by others who studied them before 1855, and area III at this time entirely escaped attention. Thus Schöll described, and Hoffer drew in his plan, merely the triangular area II which was formed by

---

[1] Ross, 1855, p. 78. Burnouf states that the remains south of the Southwest Wing were discovered in 1835 (Burnouf, 1850, pl. I:3; p. 10, note 1), but this is probably an error.

[2] The three sections are designated by letters, in different orders, by Michaelis (1876, pl. XV) and Weller (1904, pp. 36–37, pl. I):

Dinsmoor, Jr.	Michaelis	Weller
I	C	C
II	A	B
III	B	A

[3] Schöll, 1841, p. 116, note.

[4] Ross, 1855. Weller erroneously states that this was first printed in the *Tübinger Kunstblatt* at an earlier date (1904, p. 35).

the side wall and the perpendicular parastas; Hoffer represented these two walls as forming an obtuse angle, while Schöll said that the angle was acute.[5] The question of the meaning of the remains, whether they were remains of an older building or walls of a room closed on the other side, was left open. Chaudet observed the two groups I and II, but made no attempt to connect them.[6] For him, area I was possibly the earlier sanctuary of Athena Hygieia, and the structure in area II formed a doorway; in his manuscript report he conjectured that the latter was the old entrance to the Akropolis, but in his published article he decided that it was entirely covered by a staircase which led above to the Cyclopean tower. Burnouf represented both areas on his plan of 1848, not otherwise referring to the parastas, and described the structure at the south as an altar; although he discussed the older Propylaia, it was only in connection with some architectural fragments which he considered to have come from such a structure.[7] Penrose and Willson also measured areas I and II (Willson omitting the stylobate); Penrose, apparently referring to both groups, said that "these are the foundations of a structure of the nature of a Propylon . . . razed to the ground when Pericles determined on erecting the magnificent building which was designed by, or entrusted to the care of Mnesicles."[8] Penrose was thus the first to publish the identification of the remains as those of the Propylon. Beulé and Lebouteux likewise observed areas I and II (Lebouteux omitting the stylobate); although he recognized that area II was probably part of the innermost of the early entrances to the Akropolis, Beulé assumed that area I represented a separate structure, perhaps the shelter for a statue.[9] As for the date, only Burnouf, Penrose, and Beulé hazarded conjectures; Penrose considered the workmanship to be post-Persian, while Burnouf made it pre-Persian, and Beulé assigned it definitely to the age of Peisistratos.

The detailed publication by Ross was intended for the second part of his incomplete work, *Die Akropolis von Athen,* but it was not published until, after a revision in 1854, it appeared as an appendix, *Reste der vorpersischen Propyläen,* with a plan drawn by Schaubert, in his *Archäologische Aufsätze.*[10] When it finally appeared, it provided a careful plan of all three areas, I, II, and III, and described and identified the remains. Ross also made suggestions as to architectural members which might have come from the superstructure. The work by Ross remained the standard authority for the next 25 years. On it were based the descriptions and investigations of Dyer, Michaelis, Burnouf, and Robert.[11] Michaelis and Burnouf (the latter for the second time) published plans of the remains on a very small scale.

During this period no detailed restoration of the plan was undertaken. Ross suggested that if at some time the debris should be removed from the corner between the Central Building and the north wing, there would be found the continuation of the line of the rock cuttings in the central doorway and the wall corresponding to the south flank wall.[12] But this prophecy, which would have yielded a very wide structure, to be designated as the *wide* type in the following discussion, was not fulfilled. "As is now known, the actual excavation revealed nothing of the sort. The rock in the space in question proves much deeper than he thought, and the area is occupied by the large

---

[5] Schöll, 1841, p. 116, note, pl. CCCXC, fig. 3.

[6] In his unpublished mémoire of 1847, Chaudet writes: "Près du mur Cyclopéen, on trouve une partie du dallage d'un petit temple antique déjà ruiné sans doute à l'époque de la construction des Propylées. Il y a aussi un reste de porte en marbre où vient aboutir le mur Cyclopéen; c'était peut-être l'ancienne entrée de l'Acropole." See also his published report, Chaudet, 1852, pp. 297–298, and pl. 193, HH.

[7] Burnouf, 1850, pp. 10, note 1, 31–32, pl. I:3.

[8] Penrose, 1851, pp. 61–62, pl. 27.

[9] Beulé, 1853, pp. 83–84, 87–88, 178–180, 287–289, pl. 2 (b, c, d); Beulé, 1862, pp. 43–44, 85, 160, pl. 2; Beulé, 1868, p. 201.

[10] Ross, 1855, pp. 77–82, pl. IV.

[11] Dyer, 1873, pp. 128, 132. Michaelis, 1862, pl. CLXII; Michaelis, 1876, pp. 276–278, 290, 291, pl. XV; Michaelis, 1877, pp. 99–100. Burnouf, 1877, pp. 186–188, pls. VI, IX, XII (cf. pl. XVII). Robert, 1880, pp. 175–176.

[12] Ross, 1855, p. 79.

Roman cistern. These results aside, moreover, so great a width seems very improbable and not consistent with the structure of any other Greek propylaea, or even Greek building, that we know."[13]

No restorations were attempted by the other early investigators, Hoffer and Schöll, Chaudet, Penrose and Willson, or Beulé and Lebouteux. Michaelis, in 1876, interpreted the most prominent rock cutting in the central aisle of the Propylaia as being the foundation for a step on the axis of the Propylon; he avoided the difficulties of a restoration, however, and apparently treated the southwest corner of the Propylon as something extraneous. He comments that of the door at A (the anta wall) one must assume that it was a side door lying outside the main road, destined perhaps to connect the precinct of Athena Nike with the proper area of the Akropolis, but he refrains from all conjectures as to how the whole gate building was arranged.[14] Michaelis also attempted to include among the traces of the Propylon the curbstone, or water barrier, of the precinct of Athena Hygieia, a theory definitely refuted by Bohn.[15] Like Michaelis, Burnouf had the erroneous idea that the anta was a door jamb. Instead of a *wide* plan, however, he restored for the first time a plan of the *narrow* type, with a single, central doorway and a corresponding parastas and flank wall at the north.

As to the question of date, Ross assumed, because of the traces of fire, that the Propylon was pre-Persian, and in this he was followed by Dyer and Michaelis. Burnouf was more specific, and, consistent with his previous stand, accepted Beulé's theory that the Propylon was erected by Peisistratos.[16] Robert alone disagreed with other investigators of this period, following Penrose in the theory that the entire structure was post-Persian.

Some clearing of area II, east of the Southwest Wing, apparently took place in connection with the removal in 1875 of the Frankish tower which overlay the Wing. It was then that Furtwängler first observed the continuation of the marble facing of the Pelasgian wall from area I into area II (Pl. 6). He considered it, however, not as part of the Propylon but as a separate precinct of the Charites.[17]

1880–1902

The second comprehensive study of the Propylon was that undertaken by Bohn in 1879–80. He evidently did some additional cleaning in areas I and II and uncovered the "tripod base" and some of the steps parallel to the Pelasgian wall. His detailed description and drawings completely supplanted those of Ross, and formed the basis of all discussions during the following two decades.[18] New observations of isolated details, based upon study of the structure as it was left after Bohn's excavation, were made by Fabricius, Middleton, Miller, Dörpfeld, Wiegand, and Klein.[19] In 1889 the rock cuttings in area III were more thoroughly cleaned during the course of the general excavation of the Akropolis.[20]

[13] Weller, 1904, p. 51.

[14] Michaelis, 1876, pp. 277–278, pl. XV.

[15] Bohn, 1880b, p. 333.

[16] Cf. also Guillaume, 1877, p. 43.

[17] Furtwängler, 1878, p. 187, note 2.

[18] Bohn, 1880a, p. 265; Bohn, 1880b, p. 333, pl. XI; Bohn, 1882, pp. 3, 4, 16–17, pls. II, III, VIII, X.

[19] Fabricius, 1886, pp. 187–188. Middleton, 1892, pp. 15, 29, 30, 32. Miller, 1893, pp. 506–508, 519–520. Dörpfeld, 1897, p. 167, and 1902, pp. 399, 405–406, 411–412. Wiegand, 1904, pp. 50, 109–110 (cf. Schrader, 1905, p. 317). Klein, 1904, p. 321. Cf. also Milchhöfer, 1885, pp. 201, 203; Von Rohden, 1888, pp. 1415–1416, pl. LII; Bötticher, 1888, pp. 60, 88–91; Penrose, 1888, pl. 27; Harrison and Verrall, 1890, pp. 353–355; Lolling, 1889, p. 339; Wolters, 1890, p. 94; Curtius, 1891, p. 68; Middleton, 1900, pl. I (nos. 22, 23, 27); P. Gardner, 1892, pp. 254, 257; Hitzig and Blümner, 1896, p. 243; Frazer, 1898, II, p. 254; Busolt, 1897, p. 571; Bury, 1900, p. 374; Michaelis, 1901, pls. XVII, XVIII:8; E. Gardner, 1902, pp. 55–56.

[20] Kavvadias and Kawerau, 1906, cols. 135/136.

With regard to the restoration of the plan, this period is distinguished by the general adoption of what may be known as the *small square* type (Pl. 5). The original suggestion seems to have been made by Bohn, to the effect that the most prominent cutting in area III was the site of the anta diagonally opposite the anta now extant,[21] and that the distance between the two antae, and so the total width of the road, would be determined as about 8 meters.[22] This was adopted by Dörpfeld, who thus restored the outline of the Propylon as a square of 13.5 m. on each side, as in his plan of the Propylaia published in 1885 (Pl. 5).[23] Dörpfeld's plan was copied at a small scale both by Kawerau, in his drawings of the Akropolis dating from 1889[24] and 1903,[25] and by Michaelis.[26] A more detailed restoration, indicating the positions of the columns which would fit this outline, was also published by Michaelis (Pl. 5).[27] A variation of this type is that given in one of Middleton's notebooks, repeating Dörpfeld's plan, but with an amendment changing the east wall to a gate wall and adding a portico further east.[28]

Another type of plan, broader than the others, was that restored by Choisy, based, apparently, on the suggestion by Michaelis that the east-west axis of the Propylon ran through the cuttings under the great doorway of the Propylaia (Pl. 5). The *wide* type of plan which resulted has a façade of about 21 meters, and a depth from east to west of about 11.50 meters.[29]

At the beginning of the period under consideration, Bohn retained what was at that time the more traditional dating of the Propylon to the era of Peisistratos, and this was accepted by Milchhöfer. But Dörpfeld, because of a desire to associate the Propylon with the marble older Parthenon (which he at that time assigned to the Kimonian period), revived Robert's suggestion that the Propylon was post-Persian, and he definitely attributed it to Kimon. This decision was then almost universally accepted, as we may observe in the works (cited above, footnote 19) by Fabricius, Bötticher, Penrose, Harrison and Verrall, Lolling, Wolters, Middleton, P. Gardner, Busolt, Bury, E. Gardner, and Kawerau. Von Rohden, Blümner, and Frazer wavered between the two attributions. Only Miller, Curtius, and Choisy came out emphatically in favor of the Peisistratid date. Then Dörpfeld shifted to a new position; in 1897, when he decided that the older Parthenon was pre-Persian, he proposed that the Propylon also was pre-Persian and in 1902 he suggested a totally new pre-Persian date, 490-480 B.C. In this he was followed by Wiegand, Schrader, and Klein.

1903-1946

Now we come to the third period of investigation, initiated by Weller's detailed study of the Propylon. In connection with this, during the summer of 1901 he made a slight excavation in area II, which may here be described in his own words:[30]

---

[21] Weller, 1904, p. 52.

[22] Bohn, 1882, p. 16b.

[23] Dörpfeld, 1885, pl. II. Reproduced by Bötticher, 1888, p. 177; Harrison and Verrall, 1890, p. 352; Guhl and Koner, 1893, p. 106; Hitzig and Blümner, 1896, pl. VIII; Frazer, 1898, II, p. 251; Carroll, 1907, p. 273; D'Ooge, 1908, p. 172; Fowler and Wheeler, 1909, p. 156; Michaelis, 1923, p. 282; Stevens, 1936, p. 447; Hill, 1953, p. 142 (although from her reference it would seem she actually wanted to reproduce the later plan of Stevens, 1946).

[24] In Kavvadias, 1889, pl. opp. p. 50. Reproduced by Harrison and Verrall, 1890, pl. opp. p. 343; Miller, 1893, pl. XV; Guhl and Koner, 1893, p. 93; Lübke, 1899, p. 151; Middleton, 1900, pl. I; D'Ooge, 1908, plan VII; Baumgarten, Poland, and Wagner, 1913, p. 166. From the plan of 1889, the square outline was added to Kaupert's plan of the Akropolis (dating from 1879), as published by Curtius, 1891, pl. V; Gardner, 1902, plan at end; Borrmann, 1904, p. 137; Fowler and Wheeler, 1909, p. 145; Gulick, 1911, p. 49; Michaelis, 1923, p. 266.

[25] Kavvadias and Kawerau, 1906, pls. A', B'.

[26] Michaelis, 1901, pl. III.

[27] Michaelis, 1901, pl. XVII. Reproduced by D'Ooge, 1908, plan I; cf. Baumgarten, Poland, and Wagner, 1913, p. 364.

[28] Middleton, 1892, p. 15.

[29] Choisy, 1899, I, p. 412.

[30] Weller, 1904, p. 37.

Desiring to make my measurements more complete, I obtained permission, through the kindness of Mr. Kabbadias, to clear the site, with particular reference to removing the earth and rubbish which had accumulated nearly to the level of the top of the stylobate beneath the anta and had rendered it partially inaccessible. Mr. Philios, the Ephor of the Acropolis, gave me much assistance, appointing some of the regular laborers of the Acropolis to aid in the work. The appearance of the soil and the presence of iron mortar-shells were manifest proofs of the recent date of the upper layers of the earth removed. Below these, however, the soil manifestly had been in place since the time of the erection of the Propylaea [of Mnesikles], and, in fact, consisted largely of flakes from the marble of that building. In this earth were a few unimportant potsherds and some bits of lead and iron. The excavation proved, however, to be important in uncovering parts of the Propylon which had been hidden, restoring to us two fine marble steps under the stylobate of the anta, . . . a slab of the Propylon's floor (noted by Bohn, but in a wrong position), the lead-lined socket of an inscription or herm, and some minor details.

The debris which had accumulated since 1880 in area I was also cleaned out at this time, resulting in the discovery of a corner of the third poros step below the marble seat.[31] The accurate and detailed descriptions by Weller,[32] accompanied by a new set of drawings which corrected many inaccuracies in those of Bohn, formed the basis of opinion for the next few decades.[33]

The *narrow* plan, suggested earlier by Burnouf, was again evolved by Weller on the theory that the rock cuttings in the central aisle of the Propylaia (area III) mark the extreme northern limit of the structure (Pl. 5). The result was a building about 13.50 meters deep, as in most of the previous restorations, but only 11 meters wide, with only two columns between the parastades on both fronts, and with the gate wall omitted. This scheme was reproduced by most of the investigators of the period following 1904; only Kawerau, who had already prepared his latest plan of the Akropolis in 1903, although it was not published until three years later, retained the earlier *small square* type of plan for the Propylon (see footnote 25). Welter, in his drawings which were published in 1923, introduced a novel feature within the forecourt of the Propylon:[34] the thin poros orthostate at the west end of the steps in area I, south of the Southwest Wing of the Propylaia, is treated as the east wall of a tunnel which is restored with a hypothetical corresponding west wall, both of them cutting obliquely through the steps. To make this tunnel more plausible, and accessible, Welter increased its height by superposing a second course of orthostates above the one that now exists, an improbable piece of construction, and then capped these walls with a roof. After this interruption of the steps, they, along with the marble seat and metope dado, are represented as continuing further westward until they abut against a hypothetical precinct wall of Athena Nike. This restoration of a tunnel, or underground niche, seems to gave gained credence: Picard and Judeich both reproduced some of the drawings, and Picard suggested that the tunnel may be related to the chthonian cult of the Charites (comparing the entrance to the "Prytaneion" at

---

[31] Weller, 1904, p. 47.

[32] Weller, 1903, pp. 93–94; Weller, 1904, pp. 35–70, pls. I–IV; Weller, 1913, pp. 33, 226–229, with plans pp. 225, 232, 258.

[33] Judeich, 1905, pp. 62–63, 197, note 5, 198, 201, 203, 207–208, 404, and 1931, pp. 66–67, 213, note 4, 215, 218, 220–221, 225–226. Luckenbach, 1905, pp. 7–8. Harrison, 1906, pp. 12, 32, 33. Furtwängler, 1906, p. 497. Kavvadias and Kawerau, 1906, cols. 139, 140. D'Ooge, 1908, pp. 19, 31, 39, 47, 72–77, plans I, II, VII. Petersen, 1908a, pp. 19, 48–50, 95, and 1908b, pp. 27–28. Köster, 1909, pp. 20, 23–36. Collignon, 1910, p. 10, and 1914, pp. 42–43. Dörpfeld, 1911b, pp. 93–94. Fougères, 1911, p. 40, plans pp. 25, 26, 30; Fougères, n.d., p. 688; Fougères, 1914, pp. 41, 44, 46. De Sanctis, 1912, p. 314. Winter, 1912, p. 94. Beloch, 1912–1916, I.1, p. 390, II.1, p. 206. Heberdey, 1919, pp. 179–180, 230. Schede, 1922, p. 43. Welter, 1923b, pp. 507–508, and 1923a, pls. IV, V. Picard, n.d., pp. 21, 29–30, figs. 14, 27–29. Weickert, 1929, pp. 170–172.

[34] Welter, 1923a, pls. IV (in red), V:5, 6, 10 (the accompanying text contains no allusion to these features).

Thasos), while Judeich assumed that it was the seat of the cult of Hekate.[35] This tunnel, however, is so purely hypothetical, demands such peculiar construction (the superposed thin orthostates) and presumes such an awkwardly elevated westward prolongation of the steps, high above the natural rock, that it may be dismissed without further ado.

At the end of this period, in 1945, Robertson proposed the addition of a gate wall within the plan which had been proposed by Weller. He suggested "two Doric porches distyle *in antis,* before and behind a great gate in the fortress wall."[36]

In this third period of investigation the Kimonian date formerly assigned to the Propylon during the last two decades of the 19th century was definitely abandoned. Weller supported the earlier minority claims of a Peisistratid date because of the use of Z clamps in the forecourt, and he was followed in this dating by Judeich, D'Ooge, Petersen, Köster, Fougères, De Sanctis, and Beloch. The alternative, that the Propylon was erected in the decade between 490 and 480 B.C., as Dörpfeld had suggested, was adopted by Luckenbach, J. Harrison, Furtwängler, Kawerau, Collignon, Winter, Baumgarten, and Robertson. An intermediate theory, that the Propylon was erected just before 510 B.C., was preferred by Heberdey. The latter also suggested that we possess both architectural and sculptural pieces belonging to an even earlier form of the Propylon, a much wider building erected before 580 B.C., but these remains actually belong to the Hekatompedon.[37]

1946–1977

In preparation for his study of the Propylaia, Dinsmoor cleared, in May, 1910, the small area hereafter known as IV (Pl. 6), where four marble floor slabs were missing, their absence having created an accessible gap in the north aisle of the Central Building of the Propylaia.[38] This rectangular gap in the flooring had been filled with earth, except at the north end where a row of six and one-half bricks, each one about 0.35 m. square, had been installed as a repair, probably in the Byzantine period. The earth filling was not ancient and contained nothing of significance except for a marble bearded head, larger than life-size (Akropolis Museum inv. no. 4917), which was found in the deepest part (the southwest corner) and which is mentioned chiefly to prove that the cavity had never been excavated. Bedrock appeared at levels of 0.315 to 0.480 m. below the protective surface of the floor of the Propylaia; the rock had been cut to fit courses of a building which bore no relation to, and was not oriented with, the Mnesiklean Propylaia (Pl. 7; Plan A). This area, then, must also be taken into account in a study of the early Propylon. The rock here is no longer visible, the hole having been refilled to the level of the pavement.[39]

Between April 22 and May 14, 1918, Dinsmoor investigated another area, V (Pl. 6), the narrow strip, 0.758 to 0.771 m. in width, bordering the toichobate of, and lying just within, the Southwest Wing of the Propylaia; in this area the marble border slabs, which had supported marble seating,

---

[35] Picard, n.d., pp. 21, 29–30, figs. 14, 28–29 (the so-called "Prytaneion" is no longer regarded as such).

[36] Robertson, 1945, p. 89.

[37] Heberdey attributed to such a structure a group of architectural remains (H2) and also a portion of a sculptured pediment (VII Heberdey = II Buschor) from a large building which he assumed to be independent of, but dating about the same time as, the Hekatompedon (Herberdey, 1919, pp. 77–87, 136–143, 178–181). Using these remains, Heberdey assumed that his propylon had a pediment about 16.75 m. in length, containing two lionesses devouring bulls. This pediment was larger even than the one estimated by Wiegand for his main "H" temple, a restoration which Heberdey accepted (Wiegand, 1904, pp. 54–55). The existence of such a large propylon was so dubious that the proposed identification was rejected by Buschor (1922, pp. 96, 103), Weickert (1929, pp. 20, 101, 124), Schrader (1928, pp. 57, 85), Picard (n.d., p. 29), and Dinsmoor (1947, pp. 140–147).

[38] Dinsmoor, unpublished notes: "I also cleared at the same time a similar area in the south aisle, where two slabs had been removed. The spot proved to contain a small square cistern (1.57×1.80 m., and 0.42/0.50 m. deep, with a round basin in one corner), built of concrete and lined with stucco, which it was almost impossible to remove; I could only determine that the bed rock level under the west half of the cistern varies from 0.55 m. to 0.61 m. below the pavement of the Mnesiclean Propylaea. The cistern was afterwards refilled."

[39] After learning from Dinsmoor about this area, Bundgaard briefly opened it again in 1946 (Bundgaard, 1957, pp. 41–43).

had been torn out to make place for the foundations of the Frankish tower. It was hoped that this excavation would not be excessively difficult; the builders of the tower, however, had removed not only the marble border slabs and the single course of poros masonry below them, but also all of the supporting earth down to solid bedrock, which lies at depths varying from 1.24 m. to at least 2.10 m. below the pavement level, and had then refilled the cavity with solid concrete.[40] The work proved so arduous that Dinsmoor merely opened three pits at significant points, revealing two additional rock-cut steps of the forecourt of the Propylon (Plan A).[41] These three pits (V^1, V^2, and V^3), after lying open for several years, were refilled.

Stevens, in 1936, was concerned primarily with the Mnesiklean structure and merely reproduced both the drawing in Harrison and Verrall, which shows the *small square* type of plan of Dörpfeld, and also a simplified version of Weller's *narrow* plan for the Propylon.[42] Subsequently he learned of the excavation of 1910 in area IV in the north aisle. Although he was not fully acquainted with the details and mistakenly assumed that an actual trace of the north flank wall appeared in this area, he was correct in concluding that the ledge which had been found here, cut in the bedrock, demanded a wide front, with four rather than two columns between the antae. On the other hand, he followed Weller to the extent of assuming that the position of the east front of the Propylon was determined by the rock cuttings under the central doorway in the middle aisle of the Propylaia. He thus evolved, in 1946, a plan that is very shallow in proportion to its great width, about 13×17 m. (externally);[43] this was the first return to the *wide* type of plan since the one of about 13×22 m. published by Choisy in 1899 (Pl. 5). Stevens also rightly felt that a propylon should have gates (which Weller had omitted), and therefore interpolated a gate wall between the west and east fronts, with five doorways corresponding to the five intercolumniations of the façades, and with two rows of two columns each inside the west portion of the building. Noting that the level of the east front, as restored on the line of the rock cuttings, would have been higher than that of the west front, he restored three steps back of his east colonnade. In order to maintain the same height of columns on each façade, he had to raise his roof at the east end and he assumed that the gate wall, as in the Mnesiklean Propylaia, must have marked the break in the roof levels.[44] To this structure he suggests the attribution of the poros entablature that was published by Wiegand as belonging to Temple C, which had a columnar spacing of 2.304 m.; this suggestion is invalidated, however, by the difference of material and also of date (since Temple C must have been erected as early as about 550–540 B.C.), coupled with the absence of any corroborative measurements by Stevens.[45]

Bundgaard, having likewise been told of the excavation of 1910 in the north aisle, re-excavated the area in November, 1946, and correctly perceived that it revealed not the location of the north wall of the Propylon but merely a continuation of the series of rock cuttings which had been found in the central aisle, without any definite northern termination. Obviously this northern continuation demanded a wide front for the Propylon, even wider than the one which Stevens had restored; and, assuming that the rock cuttings in the central aisle of the Propylaia should be asso-

[40] The depth is certainly greater toward the northwest, but 2.10 m. was the deepest level which was actually attained.

[41] The average quantity of concrete removed in each hole was 1.50 cubic meters. The average time to clear each hole, using a marble cutter for the work, was 6 2/3 days.

[42] Stevens, 1936, p. 447, fig. 2, and pp. 467, 469, figs. 20, 22.

[43] Stevens, 1946, pp. 80–81, figs. 4, 6.

[44] His plan has been reproduced by W. Johannowski, 1958, p. 806; L. and R. Matton, 1963, p. 44; Tiberi, 1964, p. 63 (who shows this and the *large* type of plan superposed on each other, with no preference).

[45] Stevens, 1946, p. 80, note 8. The entablature of Temple C (Wiegand, 1904, pl. XIII:4), if used on the Propylon with a wide central intercolumniation, would have resulted in a total width of 0.444 + (6 1/2 × 2.304) = 15.420 m., which is far too little for the width of the building. For Dinsmoor's objections, see Dinsmoor, 1947, p. 126, note 83.

ciated with the gate wall of the Propylon rather than with the east front, Bundgaard placed the latter farther east and estimated an external depth of 17 meters, and an internal width of 17.16–17.56 m., producing a building of the *large* type of plan, nearly as large as the Central Building of the Propylaia of Mnesikles (Pl. 5).[46] He inferred that, like the present structure, there were five doorways in the gate wall and five internal steps below this wall (he later changed the number of steps to four), but he omitted any internal supporting columns.

Bundgaard did not initiate the *large* type of plan, since, based on the excavation of 1910, such a restoration had already been conceived and published in preliminary form by Dinsmoor in 1947 and 1950.[47] However, Bundgaard's more extensive treatment of the building in 1957 caught the eye of the archaeological world and his drawing was later adopted or adapted by various scholars such as Tiberi, who apparently was not fully convinced since he shows it and the Stevens plan together, superposed; Gruben; Boersma; Travlos; Hellström; Coulton.[48]

Plommer, in 1960, ignored the rock cutting in area IV and returned to Weller's *narrow* plan.[49]

Bundgaard's most recent publication suggests that the thin poros orthostate at the west end of the rock-cut steps in area I, which had been considered part of a tunnel, or underground niche, by Welter, Picard, and Judeich, indicates the south side of an entrance to the early Nike precinct.[50] Although the bedrock in front of these steps (elev. + 140.84 m.) and the ground level at the altar in front of the naïskos to the south (elev. + 140.786 m.) are almost the same, the level at the base of the poros orthostate (elev. + 141.733 m.), which would necessarily be Bundgaard's threshold, would require steps rising almost 0.90 m. and then descending the same amount again to get from one area to the other; such an idea may be dismissed.[51]

During this final period of investigation and study, the dates given for the building have been more heterogeneous than in the past, covering all conceivable periods. Stevens, in 1936, when he reprinted the drawing published by Harrison and Verrall, erased the legend "Propylaea of Kimon" which had appeared on it, and then, apparently following Weller, implied in the text a date in the second half of the 6th century B.C. (i.e. Peisistratid).[52] Later, he merely referred to it as the "entrance of the Acropolis in 437 B.C." (i.e. the gateway in use immediately prior to the Mnesiklean structure).[53] Tomlinson, in 1976, and Coulton, in 1977, concur with a Peisistratid date.[54] Berve, on the other hand, subscribed to Dörpfeld's belief in a date in the 480's, while Gruben merely states that it was after the period of the tyrants.[55] Plommer is noncommittal, stating: "Whatever its date – and it could, I think, be older than is generally thought –."[56] In 1957, Bundgaard refrained from giving a date;[57] in 1976, however, he proposed the latest, and, as will be shown, the least tenable one, when he ascribed the building of the Propylon and of the marble-lined forecourt to a homogeneously planned project carried out by Kallikrates in the period after 458/7 B.C.[58] Although unaware of the cleaning operation of 1975, which produced a still additional

[46] Bundgaard, 1957, pp. 9, 30–44, 190–192, notes 21–49, figs. 22, 28, 29, 34, 40, 41, and 1976, pp. 153–155.

[47] Dinsmoor, 1947, p. 122, and 1950, p. 197.

[48] Tiberi, 1964, p. 63. Gruben, 1966, p. 174, and 1976, p. 179; Berve and Gruben, 1966, p. 381. Boersma, 1970, p. 201. Travlos, 1971, figs. 71, 614 (also in Vanderpool, 1974, p. 158). Hellström, 1975, p. 90. Coulton, 1977, fig. 52.

[49] Plommer, 1960, pp. 146–150.

[50] Bundgaard, 1976, p. 44, note 111, pl. G.

[51] Various of Bundgaard's new ideas are discussed below, pp. 29 (footnote 57), 49–51, 57 (footnote 63), 62.

[52] Stevens, 1936, p. 447.

[53] Stevens, 1946, pp. 77, 78.

[54] Tomlinson, 1976, p. 40; Coulton, 1977, p. 119. See also Boersma, 1970, pp. 19, 21–22, 51, 68.

[55] Berve and Gruben, 1966, pp. 80, 380.

[56] Plommer, 1960, p. 148.

[57] Bundgaard, 1957. On p. 72 he labels the plan "period before 437."

[58] Bundgaard, 1976, pp. 53, 114–117.

phase in the early construction, he must have been aware that more than one building phase existed for the gate building, the total life span of which he was trying to condense into a period of 20 years.

The latest cleaning operation in the Propylon was carried out in the spring of 1975, in area II.[59] Although it provided no further knowledge of the building itself, one new discovery of importance was made when we found that the marble lining of the Pelasgian wall had originally continued further to the north than was previously known, into the area of the Propylon. Thus we have incontrovertible proof that the theatral area outside the Propylon was not constructed as a forecourt to that building but as an embellishment of the still more ancient gateway to the Akropolis.

The following measurements and notes were made at various intervals between 1910 and 1977. My reason for republishing the structure is not merely the desire to treat as a whole the development of the entrance to the Akropolis, but is based also on the fact that the new surveys and studies have made it possible to obtain more accurate measurements and knowledge of the structure than were hitherto available, therefore demanding a new architectural restoration. Finally, the question of dates has yet to be decided.

[59] Eiteljorg, 1975, pp. 94–95.

III

THE FORECOURT

THE PHYSICAL REMAINS

Below and to the west of the section of the great Pelasgian wall which had been revealed in 1840 by the excavations of Pittakis (to the east and south of the Southwest Wing of the Propylaia), there is a structure, the remains of which consist of cut bedrock, poros, and marble. As more fully revealed by the additional excavations of 1880, 1901, and 1918, the structure is seen to be Z-shaped in plan (ABCD in Pl. 2), composed of a krepidoma of at least five steps (both poros and rock cut) which supports a marble seat backed by a dado of thin marble slabs. Because, as we shall see, this construction was earlier than that of the Propylon, it was not originally a forecourt to that building. It was, however, a forecourt to an earlier gate in the Pelasgian wall and was later adapted as a forecourt to the Propylon, so the old appellation will be used to identify the area.

In 1840 Pittakis had uncovered only the uppermost members of the section to the south of the Southwest Wing (area I, Pl. 6): the broken marble dado and the marble seat of the eastern arm, and the marble seat and the topmost (fifth) poros step of the southern arm. The northward continuation of the marble dado, east of the Southwest Wing (area II), was first observed by Furtwängler after the demolition of the Frankish tower in 1875. The similar continuation of the marble seat and the existence of the "tripod base", also in area II, were discovered by Bohn in 1880; it seems that he uncovered the top of the uppermost (fifth) step in area II as well, here cut in the rock, but was undecided about its outline, which he represented as very irregular. Bohn also exposed, in area I to the south of the Southwest Wing, the poros fourth step and the top of the third step. The latter he assumed to be a poros pavement. The complete height of the uppermost, fifth step in area II to the east of the Southwest Wing was revealed by Weller in 1901; "below this is a wider (fourth) step, and just at the edge of the Propylaea's foundation are evidences of still another (the third), which is immediately lost under the Propylaea."[1] The south end of this third step in area I was also discovered by Weller, south of the Southwest Wing: "a triangle of four or five centimetres on a side is all that remains to prove its true character. Even this is left by the merest accident. It happens that one block of [the] new foundation [of the Southwest Wing] at this point retreats a trifle behind the rest. Had this block projected uniformly with its neighbors, all evidence would have been concealed."[2] The middle portion of the same third step appeared inside the Southwest Wing (area V[1]) during Dinsmoor's excavation of 1918, thus giving three points on the line of the east arm, as well as the corner to the south. The two lowest (first and second) rock-cut steps, also inside the Southwest Wing, were likewise not uncovered until 1918, and have since

---

[1] Weller, 1904, p. 43.
[2] Weller, 1904, p. 47.

been reburied. It was not until 1975 that a northern continuation of the upper (fifth) step within the confines of the Propylon was discovered.[3] This rock-cut surface was traced northwards for 3.10 m. along the line of the marble dado, from the outer face of the parastas of the Propylon to the point where it was broken away for the foundation of the Central Building of Mnesikles' Propylaia (Pls. 9, 18:b, 19:b).

The east arm of this stepped (theatral) area is the longest, 11.075 m. measured on the marble dado from the south end at B^1 to the point where it disappears under the parastas of the Propylon at A^1 (Pl. 2). With the additional continuation of 3.10 m. from A^1 to A^2 within the Propylon, there is now a preserved length of at least 14.175 m. for this arm. Since the still further northward continuation passes under the Central Building of the later Propylaia, we shall never know the over-all length of this construction, the termination of which presumably would have marked the location of the still earlier gateway and the end of this stretch of the Pelasgian wall.[4]

The marble dado is built against the foot of the Pelasgian wall, diverging from the latter line, toward the south, at an angle of about 2° 13'.[5] The southern stretch of the dado lining, A^1-B^1, outside the area of the Propylon, is now subdivided into two parts by the corner of the Southwest Wing of the Propylaia. To facilitate construction of the later building, several of the facing slabs were torn out, leaving a gap of 5.952 m.; the actual lengths of the two extant portions of the facing are 3.866 m. at the north and 1.257 m. at the south.[6] The orientation of this marble facing is *ca.* 67° 58' north of true east.

In the southern arm the marble courses are not *in situ,* and even the west end of the top poros step course at C (Pl. 8) has been cut away to make space for the Southwest Wing.[7] Restoring corner C (Pl. 2) at the intersection of the lines BC and DC, we find that C is distant 3.880 m. from the marble facing of the east arm at B. The angle ABC, between the east and south arms, is 92° 31', slightly greater than a right angle.[8] The southern arm runs therefore *ca.* 19° 31' south of true east.

Most of the short western arm has been torn out; only the corner remains, giving a length of 1.345 m. as measured from C to D on the inner side of the poros slab which is clamped to the corner of the top poros step. Again the marble construction is missing. The angle at C is 114° 35', so that the orientation of the west arm CD becomes *ca.* 45° 54' north of east.[9]

THE STEPS

The lowest worked surface of the forecourt which has as yet been uncovered is in the pit V^3 (Pl. 2, Plan A), where the deepest portion of the dressed rock drops away so rapidly toward the

---

[3] Eiteljorg, 1975, pp. 94–95.

[4] Although he was unaware of the continuation of the marble dado, Bundgaard (1957, fig. 34), solely on the hypothesis that the central gate in all periods might have occupied the same geographic position, proposed for the gate wall a location which would have fallen *ca.* 9.60 meters north of my point A^2.

[5] In my Plate 2, the outer faces of the upper part of the Pelasgian wall are represented for convenience as perfectly straight lines, 5.85 m. apart (the lower part of the west face actually recedes about 0.03–0.10 m. from the given line). The west face of the upper part of the Pelasgian wall diverges by a distance of 0.07 m. at A^1 to 0.50 m. at B^1 from the line of the face of the marble dado A^1-B^1 (as now visible).

[6] The length of the dado is difficult to measure because of the intrusion of the corner of the Southwest Wing. With regard to the measurements of the construction ABCD given in my Plate 2, it may be observed that different results have been obtained in earlier publications. Thus Bohn represents the marble facing in the east arm as a bent line, not in a single plane; this is because the present ends of the facing, nearest the corner of the Southwest Wing, are not braced and have been thrust forward by the weight behind (Bohn, 1882, pl. III). Weller represented the marble facing of the Pelasgian wall as forming a single plane (1904, pl. I). Kawerau likewise shows the marble facing as being in a single plane, but gives no measurements (Kavvadias and Kawerau, 1906, pl. H').

[7] The only extant marble member of this arm, the bench block, has been moved slightly out of place.

[8] This has generally been represented in previous plans as a perfect right angle, even when shown at a large scale, as by Willson and Penrose, Weller, and Kawerau. But Schaubert and Ross recognized it as obtuse, and Bohn's measurements on the line of the marble step (2.780 × 4.230 × 5.135 m.) would give an angle of 91° 49'.

[9] This west arm was first observed by Weller (1904, p. 48, pls. I, V), but the angle was not measured.

northwest that it seems rather to have been the summit of a ramp than an actual step (its upper extremity is at elevation + 140.84 m., 0.27 m. below the tread of the lowest step and about 0.055 m. above, i.e. almost level with, the ground level surrounding the altar of the early naïskos of Athena Nike). We assume, therefore, that the stepped structure began with the riser which terminates this ramp, at a point about 5.34 m. from the marble facing of the Pelasgian wall. Between the top of the ramp and the marble facing there is a rise of 1.513 m., accomplished in five steps averaging *ca.* 0.30 m. in height and 1.07 m. in tread width; the individual heights vary, however, from 0.220 to 0.310 m., and the widths from 0.680 to 2.020 m. (Pl. 2).

I shall describe first the two lowest steps, which were cut entirely in the native rock. These appear only in the three pits excavated in 1918, the face of the lowest, or first, step in V^3, the back of the same step (and therefore the face of the second) in V^2 and V^1, while the back of the second step (and therefore the face of the third) appears only in V^1 (Plan A).[10] The lowest step, 0.27 m. high, which is the base of the entire structure, differs from all the others in its extreme width, 2.02 m., and also in the fact that the tread is not horizontal but slopes up about 0.09 m. from front to back (Pl. 2: X–X). The step also has a slight lateral inclination, dropping about 0.04 m. from north to south in the length of 4.00 m. that was investigated. These, at least, are the measurements of the step along the east arm, parallel to the Pelasgian wall. It would seem that it did not turn westward, parallel to the south arm, although the evidence is missing since the step is broken off at a distance of about 2.10 m. from the line of the marble facing at the south. The second step, 0.23 m. high at the north and 0.22 m. high at the south end of the east arm, at its points of exposure, is only 1.05 m. wide; the top is perfectly horizontal from front to back although, like the lowest step, it has a downward slope of 0.05 m. in a length of 4.00 m. from north to south. The existence of a return parallel to the southern arm is here certain, although it is concealed by the foundations of the south wall of the Southwest Wing; we may assume that the tread of the return was about 0.355 m. wide like that of the step next above (Pls. 2, 3). In all this work, the rock is not very smoothly dressed, though the treads are footworn; the risers are quite roughly picked, and sometimes have a marked backward inclination. Several natural cavities (one in the lowest step being 0.70 m. deep) were apparently filled only with earth; no traces of inserted blocks of poros occur, and the edges of these cavities are much footworn.

The three upper steps are more nearly uniform in width of tread; along the east arm they vary from 0.755 m. to 0.81 m. at the north,[11] where they are rock cut, and from 0.78 to 0.695 to 0.84 m. at the south, where they are primarily of poros blocks; along the southern arm, where they are again of poros, they are 0.355, 0.29, and 0.84 m. in width. The top step in each case was widened to receive the marble bench. In the west arm only the third step has a visible return (of unrecoverable width), the two upper steps having been replaced by a parapet, as noted below, while the returns of the first and second are buried under the foundations of the later building. Along the east arm, the heights of the three upper steps vary from ± 0.29 m. to ± 0.29 m. (the two lower risers together equal 0.58 m.) to 0.305 m. at the north,[12] and from 0.305 m. to 0.318 m. to 0.310 m. at the south. The slight increase in heights of risers toward the south is sufficient to overcome the

[10] The tread of this second step should appear also in the small triangle of 0.06×0.11 m. mentioned by Weller, south of the Southwest Wing, if this were cleaned out.

[11] Near the north end of the top step we find a peculiarity in that this step suddenly curves forward 0.335 m., for a total width of 1.145 m., and therefore reduces the tread of the fourth step to 0.42 m. in width. The object of this increase of upper tread was to provide sufficient depth for the "tripod base", along with a step in front of it, which will be described later. The wider tread, however, continues north into the area of the Propylon, presumably to support other large dedications. The present diagonal cutting of this upper rock-cut step, just north of the "tripod base", is the result of later adjustment with the marble Propylon.

[12] The height of the top step further north, at a point under the stylobate of the Propylon, rises another 0.054 m. to 0.359 m.

downward slope, to the south, of the second and third steps to a degree whereby the top of the fifth step is nearly level.

The termination of the west end of the southern arm, which Bohn had left quite vague, was first clarified by Weller in 1904. Against the obliquely cut west end of the top step, and with its top surface flush with that of the step, was placed a vertical slab (orthostate) 0.74 m. long and only 0.22 m. thick. This slab presents toward the northwest a vertical face 0.615 m. in height, which is equivalent to the two upper risers of the steps; the slab is actually 0.64 m. high, but it rests in a channel sunk 0.025 m. into the course below. Both back and front are roughly tooled. Evidently its purpose was to cover the ends of the upper steps, forming a poros facing; we may, therefore, restore a second block to continue the parapet in the same line towards the northeast as a termination of the two upper steps (Pl. 3).[13]

The course on which the poros orthostate rests is in reality the tread of the third step; furthermore, enough of the original surface of the horizontal ledge remains to show that this third step returned, parallel to the orthostate, with a finished tread. Apparently, therefore, all three of the lower steps were returned along the west arm, parallel to the orthostates. The widths of the treads are uncertain; we may suppose that all three were equal, about 0.46 m. each, as best fits the plan (Pl. 2, Plan A). The poros third step, the southern end of which terminates 0.235 m. short of the southern end of the extant orthostate, had a length of *ca.* 1.50 m.; for the two lower rock-cut steps, which would have been allowed to die away against the rising rock at the south, the lengths must have been less.

Towards the north end of the east arm the steps apparently likewise died away, against a rock-cut ramp rising to the early gate (Pl. 3).

We have already mentioned that the two lowest steps were cut entirely from bedrock. Even the three upper steps were cut as much as possible in the living rock, poros blocks being inserted only to fill out the deficiencies in the rock, especially toward the south. At the north, the only filler of poros which was required was in the top step, in front of the "tripod base". Here, a wedge-shaped block, 0.72 m. long at its outer face and disappearing back under the base, was inserted into a slot cut into the bedrock. The slot did not need to extend down the full depth of the riser. In the southern portion, where the rock is sloping off, the treads are entirely of poros blocks except at the re-entrant angle between the eastern and the southern arms where, on the third and fourth steps, two small rectangles of exposed bedrock, 0.24×0.69 m. and 0.29×0.75 m., were maintained between inserted blocks (Pl. 8). Also the lower portion of the topmost riser in the southern half of the eastern arm is cut in bedrock for a height of 0.10 to 0.12 m., with the result that the poros blocks of the tread of the fourth step, below, abut this rock-cut riser and leave an open joint. The poros upper part of this topmost tread, therefore, is only 0.19 to 0.21 m. thick. The sparing use of poros reached an extreme with the two corner blocks of the re-entrant angle of the top step where, instead of the normal 0.75 to 0.84 m. in width of tread, these blocks were cut only 0.65 m. deep, or less, and as a result were too shallow to support the marble revetment back of them (Pl. 8). For the auxiliary supports of puddles of molten lead, see p. 23.

For the poros blocks two kinds of material were used, normal soft poros and a harder variety that resembles Kará limestone but is more yellow in color. The vertical faces of these blocks are not finished, some being entirely rough, others having drafted margins; an additional indication that this part of the work was never finished is the appearance of vertical mitered joints at the re-entrant angles of the third and fifth steps.

---

[13] See p. 11 above for Welter's interpretation that the block formed one side of a tunnel, and p. 14 for Bundgaard's suggestion that it formed one side of a propylon.

The westernmost block of the southern arm is of very irregular shape, originally quadrilateral, but with an obtuse angle of 114°35' at the west end; it subsequently assumed a pentagonal plan when a triangle (0.37×0.37×0.64 m.) was cut from the corner to make space for the foundations of the Southwest Wing (Pl. 8). This corner block is fastened to its neighbor at the east by a Z clamp 0.23 m. long. The other joints have no clamps; the single clamp was used here in order to strengthen the corner, a frequent practice in the construction of unclamped walls.[14] Likewise the orthostates of the western arm were clamped to the corner block of the top step; thus the extant orthostate has a small Z clamp, 0.17 m. in length, fastening it to the southwest corner of the step block, and the missing orthostate was probably clamped to the truncated northwest corner of the step. Two T-clamp cuttings at the edge of the rock-cut platform below the "tripod base" are evidently later, having served probably for the attachment of votive offerings (Pl. 9).

THE SEAT COURSE

Resting on the top step, and abutting directly against the "tripod base", is a marble course which, although extremely low, was apparently intended as a seat, 0.292 m. high and 0.355–0.357 m. wide. The installation of this seat reduced the available tread of the top step to 0.455–0.325 m. on the eastern arm and to 0.320 m. on the southern arm. Of this seat we possess two blocks *in situ* along the eastern arm, and also one block on the southern arm; the others were removed by Mnesikles because they would have interfered, wholly or in part, with the erection of the Southwest Wing. One of the blocks so removed still lies, on its back surface, on top of the northernmost seat block that is *in situ* (Pls. 10, 11: D–D, 24). This upturned block at the north was seen by Bohn in 1880, but by a curious error he placed its bottom at the level of the top step, as if it still lay on its original bed but had been tilted up on edge.[15] The seat block beneath it, which is *in situ,* was first observed in 1901 by Weller.[16]

The northernmost seat block *in situ* is 1.660 m. in length and fits against the lower poros block of the "tripod base", which it overtops by 0.026 m. The block above it, which now rests face upward and bottom outward, may be regarded as the second block of this same course, 1.932 m. in length; after having been dropped here by the workmen of Mnesikles, it remained undisturbed because of its inaccessible position.[17] Between this second block (restored to its proper position) and the remaining seat block at the south end is a gap of 4.247 m., which would probably have been filled by two blocks of the average length 2.123 m.; these were evidently pulled out at the order of Mnesikles and dropped south of the Southwest Wing, whence in the course of time they disappeared. The fifth block, the southern one *in situ,* had an exposed length of 1.340 m.; its total length, however, is 1.91 m. because its south end continues beyond the block which forms the return of the southern arm. This projecting end, which is supported on a ledge cut in the bedrock, is roughly hewn off. The single seat block that remains on the south arm is 1.726 m. long; the final block, at the west end of the south arm, is missing. Four of the original seven bench blocks, therefore, are still extant.

[14] Compare the earlier temple of Dionysos Eleutherios at Athens (Middleton, 1900, pl. 23 [xxxi]; Dörpfeld and Reisch, 1896, p. 15), the precinct wall of the Thessalian offering at Delphi (E. M. Gardiner and K. K. Smith, "The Group of Daochus," *AJA* 13, 1909, pl. XIV [Dinsmoor]), and the Royal Stoa at the Athenian Agora (Shear, 1971, pp. 244, 245), all with Z clamps at the corners only.

[15] Weller wrongly states that Bohn believed this block to be *in situ* (Weller, 1904, p. 43); Bohn's drawing (1882, pl. X) and text clearly indicate that the block should be turned over, his only fault being that he did not see the other block of the same course *in situ* beneath it, and placed all these marble blocks one course too high, being misled by the change in the level of the toichobate of the Southwest Wing.

[16] The block *in situ* had apparently been visible, however, ever since the excavation of 1880; it appears in Wiegand's photograph (Wiegand, 1904, p. 109), taken earlier than 1901.

[17] This was first observed by Weller, who likewise assigned the block to the second position in the course (Weller, 1904, p. 43).

The back of each seat block has a band of anathyrosis 0.06 m. high along the upper edge, while the remainder of the surface is left rough; this anathyrosis is returned along each end joint, across the upper and down the front edges. The bottom surface is also treated in joint-like fashion, with unpolished anathyroses, or bearing bands, 0.075 m. wide along the front edge and 0.05 m. wide along the rear edge, while the intermediate portion is roughly sunk, as in the Massiliot and Siphnian treasuries at Delphi.[18] The exposed back of the seat along the southern arm shows a peculiar paneled treatment with vertical ribs. The blocks were laid without dowels or clamps. A pry cutting at the bottom of the north end of the southernmost block seems to indicate, illogically, that the order of laying started with the southern one and then proceeded to the north. The fact that the marble seat, like the re-employed dado behind, is completely polished, in contrast to the unfinished poros steps, and the fact that the south end of the southern seat of the east arm extends beyond its natural limit and is roughly hewn off, lead to the inference that these marble blocks, like the dado, were taken from an earlier building (see p. 30 below).

On the north end of the southern block of the east arm, at the foot of the Pelasgian wall, there is a cutting that, inexplicably, appears to be for a door-pivot. Two other late cuttings also appear on the adjoining seat block of the southern arm.

The Dado

The existence of a marble facing, or dado, behind the benches was first made known by the discovery of the fragmentary southernmost slab of the eastern arm, during the excavations of 1840. The northward prolongation of this line into area II, where three complete slabs remain, was first observed by Furtwängler after the demolition of the Frankish tower in 1875 (Pls. 23:a, 24). The cut-down fifth slab, which runs behind the stylobate of the Propylon, was noted by Weller in 1904 (Pl. 23:b). Meanwhile, just before the turn of the century, Wiegand had made his important discovery with regard to the origin of these slabs (see p. 24 below).[19]

The dado, which rises 1.025 m. above the top of the marble seats, is formed by a series of upright marble slabs, which have a total height of 1.317 m.; the dado and seats both rest directly on the top step. The slabs form a thin revetment, the thickness of which varies from 0.06 to 0.10 m.; their outer faces diverge from the front of the Pelasgian wall by a distance increasing from 0.17 m. at the north to 0.55 m. at the south.

It is impossible to conjecture how many of these slabs originally lined the east arm of the stepped area, since the bedrock cutting for them (i.e. the top step) was cut away at the north by the Central Building of the Propylaia (Pl. 9). Progressing northwards from the southern corner, the first slab is 1.257 m. in length. There is then a gap of 5.952 m., which gives room for six more slabs, averaging 0.992 m. each. The eighth, ninth, and tenth marbles, which are complete and lie behind the extant bench and the "tripod base", have widths of 1.006, 1.162, and 1.232 m. (Pls. 2, 8, 9, 10).[20] The north end of the eleventh slab, which was cut down in height to 0.448 m. during the building of the Propylon, to the level of that structure's stylobate, was cleared in 1975 and revealed a length of 1.006 m. (Pls. 12, 18:b). From that point, the remainder of the dado was removed during the construction of the Propylon. The top step continues northward from the eleventh slab for another 0.408 m. on the same plane and then steps up 0.054 m., from which point it extends 2.150 m. before it is broken away. In this length of 2.558 m. can be placed a twelfth, thirteenth, and the beginning of a fourteenth slab. The twelfth member of the dado course was therefore

[18] Dinsmoor, 1913, pp. 12 (fig. 2), 27.
[19] First published by Dörpfeld, 1902, p. 406.
[20] Plommer gives these as 1.00, 1.14, and 1.22 m., with a height of 1.30 m. (Plommer, 1960, p. 147, note 54).

notched 0.054 m. at its bottom, near its center point, and presumably the remaining slabs to the north were cut down this same amount.

The dado was also continued westward from the south end of the east arm, almost at a right angle, by at least three slabs with a total length of about 3.40 m.; two pry cuttings, 1.23 m. apart, and a tooled bed, 1.02 m. long, indicate the allowable extremes for the length of the third, most westerly of these slabs (Pl. 8). The exact form of the west end of this facing is uncertain; it would be possible to restore a fourth slab terminating on the poros orthostate of the west arm (Pl. 3); it would also be possible, instead, that some special termination, possibly a marble pedestal as suggested by Weller, may have been devised at this point. In any case, we have the remains of five slabs and space for more than eight others on the east arm, and space for yet four more on the southern arm, indicating a minimum of eighteen in all.

The bed for the marble dado varies considerably. At the north end of the east arm the slabs rested on solid rock. Further south they rested on the poros blocks of the top step. Under the southernmost slab, however, the poros step did not extend sufficiently behind the seat to provide a support for the dado; the same situation applied as well for a length of 1.00 m. along the southern arm. Here the slabs apparently rested only on tamped earth, on which were poured at intervals small pools of molten lead to act as supports; Dinsmoor found such an irregular puddle of lead, measuring 0.077×0.093 m., *in situ* at the foot of the Pelasgian wall (Pl. 8).[21] Of the three slabs of the southern arm which assuredly existed, the easternmost rested partly on an extension of the southernmost poros block of the top step of the east arm and upon dressed bedrock, both cut down some 4 centimeters below the level of the step; its eastern corner must have been notched to fit over the prolongation of the southern seat block of the east arm (Pl. 8). The second slab must have rested partly on lead puddles, but at its west end it lapped over the second block, to the west, of the top poros step where a bed, sunk 0.035 m., was provided. The third slab rested entirely on the poros step, sunk 0.03 m. below the exposed tread.

The slabs were apparently placed after the seat blocks were installed, being dropped into the space between the seat and the Pelasgian wall and then being braced by filling the remaining interval back of the slabs with small stones and earth. No clamps were used at the top, either to connect the slabs to each other or to anchor them to the wall. In consequence of this weak construction, the slabs, which were originally vertical, now have marked forward inclinations, amounting to 0.039 m. at the northernmost, 0.064 m. at the central one, and 0.095 m. at the southernmost of the complete slabs. For the south arm there is at present no indication of a backing wall, although some sort of support for the slabs must have existed. At one place, behind the extant bench block of this arm, the bedrock was chiseled down only to a level 0.023 m. higher than that of the top step to help give support for such backing (Pl. 8).

Above the marble slabs there may have been a low projecting coping, serving as an architectural finish and also concealing and protecting the fill behind the slabs, but this idea is doubtful. The Pelasgian wall slopes outward and in places overhangs the original line of the slabs. This outward batter is obviously not the result of later disturbances and therefore precludes the idea of any yet higher facing of the wall, other than a possible low coping. Above the dado, the rough Pelasgian wall was left visible for the remainder of its height.

Various scratched oblique lines on the slabs of the dado seem not to have any significant meaning. The topmost of these lines appears only on the two southern of the three complete slabs, rising from a point 0.225 m. below the top at the south to 0.128 m. below the top at the north, in a

---

[21] It is just north of the southernmost dado slab *in situ,* 0.290 m. below the top of the marble seat; he immediately reburied it (May 27, 1918).

length of 2.168 m.; Wiegand suggested that the scratch indicated the line of an old approach,[22] but it seems improbable that at any period before the construction of the Mnesiklean Propylaia the level could have been so high. A similar line appears on the same two slabs, 0.310 m. (at the south) to 0.348 m. (at the north) below the upper line.

Besides the sloping incised lines, the southernmost of the three complete slabs shows an almost horizontal line 0.198 to 0.212 m. below the top; it slopes only 0.014 m. in the total width of the slab (1.006 m.), and does not continue on either of the two other slabs. Below this are faint traces of at least ten incised leaves of Doric pattern, 0.062 m. wide and spaced 0.078 m. on centers; there must have been thirteen leaves in all, before they were carefully erased in order that the slab might be re-employed in its present position. Such a slab, as Wiegand remarked, could only have been one of the metopes of the old Hekatompedon, which was erected between 570 and 566 B.C.[23] No traces of such a pattern remain on the two other complete slabs, though the northernmost shows an exceptional amount of chiseling on the lower part, behind the seat, as if here, too, the ornament had been removed.[24] The fragmentary slab at the south end of the series also shows, at the present bottom, a few traces of the erased ornament.

THE METOPES: RESTORATION AND DISPOSITION

Let us first turn to two marble slabs which are most certainly part of the same series as those used in the forecourt, but which were not found in conjunction with them. These two metope slabs are the ones which bear the famous Hekatompedon inscription (E.M. 6794 = *IG* I^2, 3, 4). Along with other telling characteristics such as size, type of marble, and surface treatment, the more complete of these metopes (*IG* I^2, 4) bears the same incised leaf ornament and lower band below the fascia which appears on the third complete metope from the north in the forecourt (right side up) and on the last one at the south (upside down). It is now generally accepted that all of these slabs originated with the Hekatompedon of 566 B.C., as recognized first by Wiegand when he noticed the chiseled-off fascia and the leaf ornament which had been rubbed until it had more or less disappeared on the southernmost of the three complete slabs in the forecourt of the Propylon.[25] The more complete slab (*IG* I^2, 4), composed of 25 fragments,[26] preserves the complete cut-down width of 1.023 m.;[27] the maximum height is now only 1.165 m., with the original top (now the bottom) broken off, but it is possible to estimate that the original height of the metope was 1.325 m.[28] The other slab (*IG* I^2, 3), composed of 20 fragments, is too poorly preserved to allow restoration of its dimensions.

---

[22] Wiegand, 1904, p. 110.

[23] This identification, first published by Dörpfeld (1902, p. 406), and later by Wiegand (1904, p. 110), was then generally accepted, as it still is today. Cf. Schrader, 1905, p. 317; Judeich, 1905, pp. 62, note 12, 208, and 1931, pp. 66, note 6, 226; D'Ooge, 1908, p. 72; Petersen, 1908a, p. 49; Fougères, 1911, p. 40. Weller alone objected to this, because of a misapprehension that Wiegand was referring to the metopes of the Peisistratid temple (1904, p. 44, note 1). Judeich (1905, p. 208, and 1931, p. 226) erroneously identified these metopes as belonging to the south flank of the Propylon. For the date 570–566 B.C. assigned to the Hekatompedon, see Dinsmoor, 1947, p. 110. Beyer and Preisshofen (1977, pp. 74–77) are now trying to place the H-architecture and the metopes on an earlier temple on the old Athena-temple foundations with the very early date of 625–600 B.C.

[24] Wiegand assumed that these two metopes rest on what were originally their sides (Wiegand, 1904, p. 110); but in none of the metopes of the Hekatompedon was the width so great as the present height of the slabs, 1.317 m.

[25] Wilhelm, 1898, p. 488; Dörpfeld, 1902, p. 406; Wiegand, 1904, p. 110; Schrader, 1905, p. 317.

[26] Wiegand, 1904, p. 111, fig. 114; cf. Wilhelm, 1898, pl. IX:2; Spaulding, 1906, p. 398; Kern, 1913, pl. 13; Bundgaard, 1976, fig. 74.

[27] The exposed width, from the painted pattern, was 1.008 m. (Dinsmoor, 1947, p. 143).

[28] From the present top to a horizontal incised line marking the beginning of the ornament the height is 1.010 m.; the height of the leaves and the band below them is 0.082 m., and thence to the fascia 0.013 m.; thus the flat portion of the metope was 1.105 m. high. We add to this the fascia, normally 0.220 m. (see p. 26 below), and we have a complete height of about 1.325 m.

Wiegand was also the first to suggest that the two inscribed metopes may have been set in the forecourt along with the others which lined the Pelasgian wall.[29] He writes that he might, after this discovery (that the metopes originated in the Hekatompedon), assume that the original standing place of the Hekatompedon inscription was the platform before the old Propylon; on entering the citadel one would then be reminded of the regulations to be observed in the sacred grounds. The uniformity of treatment of the two sets, with the fascia removed and the leaf ornament rubbed down, seemingly corroborated Wiegand's supposition and this interpretation has been generally accepted. There is, however, one detail wherein these two inscribed slabs differ, both from the originally cut metopes and from the reworked ones which were subsequently employed in the forecourt. Although both sets of re-used slabs have had their vertical edges reworked and do not retain, as do the pristine metope fragments,[30] the somewhat irregular and roughly picked original edges that had been hidden behind the overlapping triglyphs, the inscribed metopes lack the chamfered lateral edges that were cut on the retrimmed slabs of the forecourt. On the more fragmentary slab (IG I^2, 3) both vertical edges were smoothly worked back to the broken rear surfaces, which are split off at a depth of 0.05 m. on one fragment of the left edge and at a maximum depth of 0.07 m. on three fragments of the right edge; the outer corners are quite square, without the characteristic chamfer, at least on the left hand fragment and on one of those at the right (the two others are abraded here).[31] On the more complete slab (IG I^2, 4), the two fragments of the left edge show a smooth margin of 0.005–0.007 m. which is followed first by a band, 0.03–0.035 m. wide, of toothed chiseling in the same plane and then by a roughly picked surface; the three fragments of the right edge show a band of coarse toothed chiseling, about 0.025 m. wide but with a poorly defined inner edge, which again is followed by a roughly picked surface; on all five of these fragments the chamfer is missing. The upper edges of the three fragments of the top of this slab are roughly tooled, with toothed chiseling appearing on the upper right corner piece; again there is no chamfer. On the rough surface of the vertical right edge of this upper right corner piece there is a slight protrusion, which implies that the accepted sequence IG I^2, 3 + 4 is to be preferred for the position of the slabs and their inscriptions; if the order were reversed (4 + 3) the common joint would necessarily be slightly open, unless we make the improbable assumption that IG I^2, 3 had a corresponding hollow on its upper left edge.[32]

The lack of chamfered lateral corners most certainly implies that the two metopes with the Hekatompedon inscription were not set up as part of the series in front of the entrance to the Akropolis, tempting as the idea is. Also, the presence of toothed chiseling, which is preserved on IG I^2, 4, proves that the edge treatment of these two slabs is not original, but dates from the period of recutting in 485/4, since the toothed chisel was unknown at the period of the erection of the Hekatompedon.[33] It does not appear at all in the early poros work on the Akropolis,[34] and its

---

[29] Wiegand, 1904, p. 110.

[30] E.g., the eleven fragments illustrated by Wiegand, 1904, figs. 14a, 14b, and 115.

[31] The right-hand fragment with the good edge is now only 0.032 m. thick, the greater thickness of 0.07 m. appearing in the two less well preserved pieces.

[32] For the absence of the chamfer and the roughness which prevents a close joint, see Dinsmoor, 1942, p. 208, and 1947, p. 119. B.   Hill had suggested that the reverse sequence IG I^2, 4 + 3 should be adopted, with fragment y transferred from the bottom of IG I^2, 4 to that of IG I^2, 3 (1906, p. 82; cf. Paton, 1927, p. 439, note 2; Dinsmoor, 1947, p. 118, note 39). Hill later wrote to Dinsmoor, however, that he was no longer so certain of this interchange of the two slabs; and certainly the presence of the rough projection would favor the order as published in IG I^2.

[33] Dinsmoor, 1947, pp. 116–117.

[34] Heberdey, 1919, p. 188. The so-called exceptions, two carelessly executed poros masks (Wiegand, 1904, p. 231, figs. 246, 247; Dickens, 1912, nos. 11, 12) and an equally rude relief (Heberdey, 1919, p. 124, fig. 135) are to be assigned, therefore, not to a primitive period (as Lechat assumed, 1891, p. 314, and 1904, p. 23, note 2), but rather to inexperienced carvers of a later time (Wiegand, 1904, pp. 231–232; Heberdey, 1919, pp. 123, 125, 188).

absence and presence, respectively, are distinctive characteristics of the Knidian (*ca.* 560–550 B.C.) and the Siphnian (*ca.* 530–525 B.C.) treasuries at Delphi.[35] Only in marble sculpture does it seem to have appeared about the middle of the 6th century, *ca.* 560 B.C.[36]

All of the metopes which were utilized in the forecourt of the Propylon were carefully reworked. The projecting top fascia was chipped off and the upper portion of the surface of the metope was rubbed and polished until the traces of the fascia and of the incised ornament below it had practically disappeared. It does not seem probable that much of the height of the metopes was cut away. If such a reduction had taken place, the discarded portion would naturally have been the original top with its fascia, which required special trimming, since the bottom already presented a smooth surface; yet, in the only accessible example, the height of the cut-down fascia (which varies from 0.215 to 0.225 m. on other, untrimmed fragments) remains almost intact, 0.199 m. at the left and 0.185 m. at the right,[37] the slab having been set up slightly out of plumb and then leveled off. There remains for the plane surface below the fascia a maximum of 1.132 m., which accords nearly with that estimated on the metope which bears the Hekatompedon inscription (about 1.105 m.; see footnote 28, p. 24). We may assume from this slab that the original height of these metopes, and so of the triglyph frieze of the Hekatompedon, was about 1.132 + 0.220 = 1.352 m.,[38] and that in the course of re-erection they were cut down about 0.035 m. The widths also were slightly altered. The originally rough lateral edges of the metopes, once covered by the edges of the triglyphs, were not suitable for exposed joints. In the slabs intended for the decoration of the forecourt, therefore, the lateral edges were smoothed, and, in addition, received a bevel 0.007 m. wide and 0.004 m. deep on the outer lateral corners. Apparently the reduction in width was not great.

In the frieze of the Hekatompedon there were evidently four sizes of marble metopes, with calculated exposed widths on the front façade of 1.172 m. (four), 1.12 m. (two), and 1.06 m. (two), and on the flanks of 1.01 m. (thirty-six).[39] Allowing margins of 0.025–0.05 m. for the edges which were concealed in the triglyph slots, we might estimate that the total original widths were about 1.222–1.272 m., 1.17–1.22 m., 1.11–1.16 m., and 1.06–1.11 m. Let us label these groups consecutively A, B, C, and D. Along the east arm of the forecourt, it is clear that the southernmost metope of 1.257 m. belongs to the widest type, A. To the gap of 5.952 m. can be assigned six metopes of 0.992 m. each, of type D. The four metopes north of the gap, of 1.006, 1.162, 1.232, and 1.006 m., are from types D, B, A, and D. On the southern arm, the eastern space between the corner return and the tooled bed at the west is 2.38 m. and can accommodate two slabs of 1.22 m. and 1.16 m., types A and B. The tooled bed for the third metope has a length of 1.02 m., for a slab of type D. Thus we have places for the following: type A, 3 of the original 4; type B, 2 of the original 2; type

---

[35] Dinsmoor, 1913, p. 8.

[36] Casson, 1937, p. 107; Adam, 1966, p. 19.

[37] The visible incised line on this third (from the north) of the complete metopes is that of the tops of the leaves, 0.013 m. below the fascia.

[38] Wiegand assumed that the original height of the metopes was about 1.40 m. (Wiegand, 1904, p. 110), of which about 0.03 m. was sunk in the epistyle, leaving 1.37 m. exposed (*ibid.,* pp. 7, 23, 46). A triglyph built up from many fragments gives a height of 1.392 m., of which he assumed that only 0.022 m. was sunk in the epistyle (*ibid.,* pp. 7, 44). But the cuttings in the epistyle below the triglyphs vary in depth from 0.133 m. (*ibid.,* p. 2, fig. 4, assuming that the original height of the taenia was 0.174 m. as pp. 5, fig. 7, and 41, figs. 57:c and 57:d) to 0.04 m. (*ibid.,* p. 41, fig. 57:c). Very rarely do we find depressions for the metopes (as *ibid.,* p. 4, fig. 6, sunk about 0.045 m.); and those that exist probably contained the few poros metopes which were cut on the triglyph slabs. The purpose of the depression was evidently to form a mortise in which should rest the base of the triglyph slab, which was here a simple facing, either constructed in one piece for the entire height (*ibid.,* p. 44), or jointed with a tongue-and-groove at half the height (*ibid.,* p. 7, nos. 38, 42, 45, fig. 10); in either case it was secured at the top to the backing by clamps (*ibid.,* fig. 8). Thus, with both top and bottom fastened, the triglyphs in turn gripped the metope slabs on either side; the marble metopes did not, therefore, require mortises.

[39] Dinsmoor, 1947, pp. 141–143.

D, 9 of the original 36. Aside from these fourteen metopes, another of type D can be placed at the west end of the southern arm, and a minimum of three others (and certainly considerably more than that) can be placed at the continuation of the north end of the eastern arm.[40]

THE DATE OF THE FORECOURT

The problem of the date of the forecourt has usually been considered as identical with that of the date of the Propylon itself; both structures have generally been treated as parts of the same design, variously attributed to Peisistratos, Themistokles, Kimon, or even Perikles. Köster alone made a sharp distinction between the two elements, assigning the Propylon to Peisistratos, but dating the forecourt, because of the freshness of the marble metopes and benches, to the later period of Kimon.[41] Weller had already made a similar distinction between the Propylon and the forecourt, on the basis of internal evidence (the relationship of the parastas to the cut-down metope of the forecourt),[42] but without any definite difference of date. The opposite to his conclusion of priorities would have been more logical, however, and from the discovery in 1975 that the metope slabs originally continued further north than the ones that are still visible, i.e. into the area of the Propylon, it is now obvious that the forecourt is the older of the structures.

The evidence for the dating of the forecourt rests almost entirely on the secondhand metopes from the Hekatompedon which were used for the marble dado lining the Pelasgian wall. In earlier studies of the forecourt, however, the use of Z clamps on the top step of the southern arm was one of the main criteria for the date.[43]

The only structural clamps visible in the forecourt, the two at the southwest corner of the top step, are of the Z form. The period of use for such clamps was regarded some years ago as being *ca.* 540–527 B.C., in that they were transitional between the dovetail clamps, which were employed on earlier buildings such as the Hekatompedon and the poros buildings "A", "B", and "C" on the Akropolis,[44] and the double-T form, which was firmly established in Athens after the death of Peisistratos, when it appeared in structures such as the altar dedicated to the Pythian Apollo by the younger Peisistratos,[45] the Peisistratid temple of Athena (superstructure),[46] the small poros building "E" on the Akropolis,[47] the early Olympieion (krepidoma),[48] the older Parthenon (krepidoma and wall base),[49] etc. More recent evidence, however, shows that while Z clamps may have been

[40] In addition to the 18 metopes accounted for here, at least 7 others, which were not employed in the forecourt, are known. Two of these are the ones on which was carved the Hekatompedon inscription, and the more complete of these can definitely be assigned to the smallest series, type D, from the flank of the temple (from the five preserved leaves, which are 0.054 m. wide and 0.0672 m. on centers, fifteen leaves can be restored on the preserved width of the metope of 1.023 m., giving 0.995 m. across the outer edges of the end leaves, and a total exposed width for the face of the metope of 1.01 m.). The other 5 metopes (or possibly even more) are indicated by the 11 fragments described by Wiegand (1904, pp. 10–12, 110–112). Thus, of the original 44 marble metopes of the Hekatompedon, from one façade and two flanks (Dinsmoor, 1947, pp. 141–143), we can make some accounting of 25.
[41] Köster, 1909, p. 29.
[42] Weller, 1904, p. 67: "the priority of the construction of the anta to that of the wing is obvious from the blending and interlocking of the steps of the wing with those of the Propylon, no less than from the fact that one of the slabs of the wing actually runs under the corner of the parastas."
[43] The importance of this form of clamp in the question of the date was emphasized by Weller, 1904, p. 67; cf. Judeich, 1905, pp. 7, 404. Bohn had previously represented the larger clamp as of double-T form (1882, pl. III).
[44] Wiegand, 1904, pp. 5, 8, 16, 23, 40, 54, 155.
[45] The inscribed crowning molding, *IG* I², 761, where the half-clamp cuttings are 0.095 m. long and 0.017 m. deep, and the heads 0.045 m. wide. See Travlos, 1971, pp. 100–102.
[46] Wiegand, 1904, p. 121.
[47] Wiegand, 1904, p. 168.
[48] Welter, 1922, p. 63, pl. 8.
[49] Hill, 1912, pp. 539, 540, 553.

transitional in origin they continued in use along with the double-T clamp, probably because they were less expensive to fabricate. Thus we find the Z clamp in the Royal Stoa in the Athenian Agora, clamping the anta to the flank wall (*ca.* 540 B.C., along with dovetail clamps): in the temple of Aphaia at Aigina, intermixed with double-T forms (*ca.* 495–485 B.C.); in the Marathon base beside the Athenian treasury at Delphi, in the front row of foundation blocks, with double-T clamps in the rear row (490); in the lower Tarentine base at Delphi (*ca.* 490–485); in the Argive niche of the Epigonoi at Delphi (*ca.* 482); in the Argive base of the Seven against Thebes at Delphi (*ca.* 456); in the Hephaisteion, for the ceiling coffer frames, with double-T clamps below (*ca.* 449); in the temple of Apollo at Bassai, in the upper portions, with double-T clamps below (*ca.* 425); in the Thessalian niche of Daochos at Delphi (after 373); in the temple of Ammon Zeus in Kallithea on the Kassandra peninsula of the Chalkidiki, in the euthynteria and krepidoma courses, with double-T clamps below (end of 4th century).[50] It is now obvious, therefore, that the Z clamps, which Weller regarded as decisive for a Peisistratid date of the forecourt, can be of little aid for dating purposes.

The metopes from the Hekatompedon, however, are more helpful for the dating. This poros temple of *ca.* 566 B.C.,[51] which was the source of the secondhand marble slabs lining the forecourt, was thought by many scholars to have been demolished about 529 B.C. to make way for the Peisistratid temple of Athena.[52] The theory was based on the assumption that the Hekatompedon had rested on either (a) the inner blue foundation or (b) the outer pink foundation of the Peisistratid temple. With such an argument, the metopes from the Hekatompedon would have been available for the embellishment of the forecourt of the entrance to the Akropolis any time after 529 (or 525) B.C.[53] This argument, however, was completely altered by Dinsmoor's demonstration, with respect both to dimensions and to technique, (a) that the Peisistratid foundations are not only too small internally but too large externally for the Hekatompedon, (b) that even if the width of the Hekatompedon were slightly increased, its solid flank walls could not have rested on the foundations of the open Peisistratid peristyle, and (c) that the pervasive use of the toothed chisel on both inner and outer foundations of the Peisistratid temple in any case forbids us to superpose on them the architectural and sculptural members of the Hekatompedon which were finished by means of an older technique, in which the toothed chisel was still unknown.[54] The Hekatompedon must therefore have stood on a totally different site, and the only one available was that of the older Parthenon. Since it was equally possible to demonstrate that the present foundation for the older Parthenon was not begun until 488 B.C.,[55] it became evident that the demolition of the Hekatompedon, of which most of the discarded remains lay in the terrace fill deposited south of the Parthenon foundations, occurred in 489 B.C., after the battle of Marathon, and so forty years later than the date previously suggested.[56] In accordance with this dating, the forecourt at the entrance to the Akropolis with its facing composed of metopes from the Hekatompedon should be assigned to 489 B.C., or shortly thereafter (if the metopes can be shown, as they will, to have been an

[50] For an earlier comment on the matter of these clamps, see Dinsmoor, 1942, pp. 200–201, 207, notes.

[51] See footnote 23, p. 24 above.

[52] This theory is still held by some scholars. See Plommer, 1960, pp. 150, 159, and Beyer and Preisshofen, 1977, pp. 74–77. The latter try to push the temple back to 625–600 B.C.

[53] Preisshofen (Beyer and Preisshofen, 1977, p. 77) even suggests that the Hekatompedon inscription might go back to the Peisistratid period.

[54] Dinsmoor, 1947, pp. 110–127.

[55] Dinsmoor, 1934, pp. 408–441; Dinsmoor, 1935, pp. 508–509; Dinsmoor, 1937, pp. 3–13; Dinsmoor, 1939a, pp. 205–206; Dinsmoor, 1939b, pp. 119–123, 134–135, 169; Dinsmoor, 1942, pp. 205–206; Dinsmoor, 1947, p. 123.

[56] Bundgaard (1976, p. 53), however, ascribes the foundation of the older Parthenon, along with various other Archaic structures, to Kallikrates after 458/7 B.C.

integral part of the original design of the forecourt), a date at which Z clamps were still very much in use.[57]

Corroboration for the date of the demolition of the Hekatompedon is given by the two marble metopes which bear the famous Hekatompedon inscription (*IG* I², 3, 4). The numerous fragments from which these slabs have been reconstructed were discovered, so far as their provenance has been recorded, in the debris of the Persian destruction, suggesting that they were broken up in 480 B.C.;[58] this provenance would accord with the freshness of the surfaces and the preservation of the red color in the letters. Consequently, the inscription should be earlier than 480 B.C. Comparison with surviving pre-Persian inscriptions indicated to Wilhelm that the lettering closely resembles that of the first two lines of the Marathon base of 489 B.C. (*IG* I², 763 + Agora I 303[59]); the lettering, in fact, seems to have been carved by the same stonecutter. The forms of the letters, and the individualistic punctuation with a vertical row of three tiny circles with central dots, are identical with those of the Hekatompedon inscription.[60] The additional third and fourth lines of the Marathon base, engraved within a band which was caused by a subsequent smoothing of the normally stippled surface, are more carelessly lettered, although they certainly antedate the destruction of the monument by the Persians in 480 B.C. Thus a date in the 480's for the demolition of the Hekatompedon and the availability of the metopes for the carving of the Hekatompedon inscription is still further strengthened.

The decisive factor in the dating of the inscription, if the restored order of the fragments is correct, is the name of the archon which appears upon them.[61] *IG* I², 3 contains the letters Φ . . . . . . Oʒ on lines 16 and 17, and *IG* I², 4 has ἐπ]ὶ Φ . . . . on a single line, 26. The second appearance of this name, because of the stoichedon system employed, definitely requires ten letters in its restoration if the vital fragment which contains the Φ is correctly placed, as it probably is, and the preceding ἐπ]ὶ is important for identification of the next word as the name of an archon and hence the word that follows the name as ἄρχοντ]ος. Examination of the Athenian archon list between 500 and 480 B.C. reveals only one name with the initial Φ, Φιλοκράτης (or Φιλοκράτος in the genitive) of 485/4 B.C., and it happens that the name is spelled with ten letters.[62] Hence, for

---

[57] Bundgaard (1976, p. 118) suggests that the Hekatompedon not only stood on the Peisistratid foundations, *but that it remained standing* there as part of a composite temple, with a later peristasis, *until the destruction of 480 B.C.* by the Persians. On his page 53 he states that Gb 1 (the Propylon) and the contemporary layout of the west ascent were the work of Kallikrates (*post* 458/7). He therefore places the construction of the forecourt *post* 480 B.C., and presumably in the 450's. In order to bolster this argument for a post-Persian construction he states that the Persian destruction level passes under the steps of the façade of the Propylon (Bundgaard, 1974a, p. 48), but the existence of Persian debris here was never noted by anyone else. It would seem that both Plommer and Preisshofen prefer much earlier dating. The former (1960, p. 150) again revives the idea that the H-fragments came from a temple of the early 6th century, placed on the old Athena-temple foundations, and dismantled *ca.* 525 B.C. The latter (Beyer and Preisshofen, 1977, pp. 75-77), who believes in this same provenance for the Hekatompedon architecture, makes the temple still earlier, 625-600 B.C., again replaced in the Peisistratid period. Both, therefore, would have the metopes available at an early date.

[58] According to Lolling (1890b, p. 92 = 1890a, p. 627), the fragments were discovered scattered practically over the entire Akropolis, beside the Propylaia, the north and south walls, south of the Parthenon, and beside the Museum; they lay in the strata of earth and stones with which the natural inequalities of the Akropolis plateau were filled and leveled up in the times after the Persian wars.

[59] H. A. Thompson, *The Athenian Agora, A Guide,* 3rd ed., Athens 1976, p. 248.

[60] Wilhelm, 1898, p. 490; Spaulding, 1906, p. 398; Oliver, 1933, pp. 480-494; Dinsmoor, 1942, p. 201.

[61] Raubitschek and I examined the fragments together in 1977, and we are bothered by the present restoration of *IG* I², 3. Line 16 is shown with 39 spaces and line 18 with 42, while the second slab has 38 spaces throughout. He correctly said that in line 18 the restoration ΤΕ(ΙΑΓΟΡΑΙΤΕΙΕΜΠ)ΟΛΕΙ is without foundation and that ΤΕ(ΙΑΚΡΟΠ)ΟΛΕΙ or ΤΕ(Ι----Β)ΟΛΕΙ might be possibilities, thus reducing the number of spaces from 42. No matter how this line is treated, however, the entire inscription needs restudy, working with the actual fragments, since one change leads to another (a new edition, *IG* I³, is now in press). There are various punctuation mistakes in the restoration of *IG* I², 3. Raubitschek definitely asserts, however, that, regardless of who the archon might be, the letter forms force one to place the inscription between 489 and 475 B.C.

[62] On inadequate grounds, merely because the archon's name is absent from the dating formulas of most 5th-century decrees, Luria (1927, pp. 257-275) has suggested that the date should be earlier than the reforms of Kleisthenes in 506 B.C. This was momentarily accepted by Dörpfeld (1929, p. 1247), while Judeich could not decide between the two dates (1929, p. 393, and 1931,

this inscription, it seems probable that we have the date 485/4, only four years later than the demolition of the Hekatompedon, giving us a fixed point in time for the availability of the metopes for use as the lining of the forecourt.[63]

On the accepted basis that the metopes which line the forecourt originated in the Hekatompedon, with the conclusion that this temple was located on foundations beneath those of the Parthenon and was demolished in 489/8 B.C. to make way for the platform of the older Parthenon, thus making the metopes available, and with the evidence from the Hekatompedon inscription carved on two of these slabs (their provenance of finding, their freshness, their letter forms, and their inclusion of the archon Philokrates of 485/4 B.C.), it appears that the only logical date for their incorporation into the forecourt, which preceded the construction of the Propylon (as we shall see, also of the 480's), was in the very early years of the decade, presumably 489/8 B.C.

A 6th-century, or Peisistratid date for the construction of the stepped forecourt itself might appear plausible if the steps could be considered as having been planned and executed without the accompanying adornment of the metopes and benches; we have already concluded that the metopes were unavailable for re-use at this early a period, and it is quite certain that the benches were equally unavailable so early since the beautifully cut marble seats could hardly have originated in the early 6th century, a date which would be necessary in order for them to have been free for re-use in the Peisistratid period. We do know that the "tripod base" was an integral part of the original design since otherwise there would be no reasonable explanation for the bulging out of the top step at the point where the base rests. But the base is hard to date.

Let us now look at the back edge of the top step. This edge is extremely ragged, especially along the southern part of the east arm where the poros blocks are of different depths. If there had not been bench blocks to hide these ragged lines, the construction would have presented a most unsightly appearance. One must suppose, therefore, that the ragged back of this step was considered immaterial since it was to be covered; and the only possible covering consists of the seat blocks which, incidentally, align with the "tripod base". One is also forced to assume that the installation of the metopes was simultaneous with the placing of the benches since the southern-most bench of the east arm was not cut down to align, and form a neat angle, with the back of the benches of the south arm but extends most carelessly considerably beyond this line; the sloppy work was ignored, however, since the easternmost metope of the south arm concealed it. Also, aside from the fact that the metopes were needed as a backrest behind the seats, which diverged from the Pelasgian wall by as much as 0.55 m., a ledge, which acted as the support for the metopes, was too conveniently provided behind the benches, at the time of their installation, to have been accidental. It therefore appears that the entire construction must have been simultaneous, as is generally accepted.

I have already mentioned the difficulty of finding an original provenance for the benches in the early- or pre-Peisistratid period. As for the eighteen or more fresh metopes which were used behind

---

pp. 70, 260); but De Sanctis opposed any date other than 485/4 (1927, p. 565). Most recently Bundgaard (1976, p. 114), in his attempt to assign various of the early buildings on the Akropolis to Kallikrates, suggests that the archon should be Φρασικλῆς (or Φρασικλέος in the genitive), 460/459 B.C.

[63] If the view is maintained that the Hekatompedon did not occupy the site of the Parthenon and did not remain standing until 489 B.C., but that the building was dismantled earlier, it could be argued that the metopes which line the forecourt were also erected earlier and that the metopes on which the inscription was carved, and the other metopes which were found in fragmentary form on the Akropolis, had been stored in the meantime until the 480's in a stockpile, but this idea does not seem very convincing, especially when one considers the metopes of the forecourt in conjunction with their attendant marble benches, which would be difficult to ascribe to the early 6th century (see below).

the benches,[64] a case has already been made that their availability for re-use here could hardly have been earlier than 489 B.C. Such a time period also allows a more acceptable later date for the original use of the benches, which may also have been associated with some construction underlying the old Parthenon. Since it appears that the construction of the steps and the installation of the benches and metopes all occurred at the same time, it follows that the entire forecourt was most likely constructed immediately after the demolition, in 489 B.C., of a Hekatompedon which underlay the old Parthenon. This construction, then, along with that of the "ground breaking" for the old Parthenon, would constitute the beginning of a new building program by the enthusiastic Athenians very shortly after the victory at Marathon.

THE "TRIPOD BASE"

The "tripod base", located at the juncture of the rock-cut forecourt and the right, front corner of the Propylon, held a place of prominence.[65] It is certainly contemporary with the steps below it, since the top step was given an excessive width at this point, curving out around the base in such a manner as to verify a single, unified scheme (Pls. 9, 24). Its back aligns with that of the adjacent marble bench and, in similar fashion to the bench, buttresses the marble metope slabs behind. In other words, it is part of the original construction of the forecourt, of about 489 B.C. Because of this, however, since it preceded the building of the Propylon and since the rock-cut step of this period continued on to the northeast, the base did not terminate the original construction. What lay beyond we shall never know, but since the widened step continued, there were probably additional votives rather than another bench. Nevertheless, even in the first period of the forecourt, the "tripod base" held a prominent position, since it was the first dedication to be viewed, terminating as it did the line of seats. Its importance is augmented in that the builders of the krepidoma of the Propylon carefully and skillfully incorporated it into their design.

The base is composed of two blocks, almost square in plan. The lower, of poros, 0.267 m. high and 0.842×0.805 m. in plan, is set with one of its longer faces aligning with the back of the marble seat described above, while the front face aligns with the riser of the rock-hewn top step further west. The upper block, of marble, 0.726×0.692 m. in plan, has a visible height of 0.223 m. but is set down on the lower block in a socket and secured with molten lead, leaving margins of 0.062 m. on the front and east side, 0.054 m. on the west side, and 0.051 m. at the back. Both stones are smoothly dressed except at the back, where the upper block, at least, is rough; they bear no traces of inscriptions. On the upper surface of the marble block are three circular sockets, 0.132–0.136 m. in diameter, at the apices of an equilateral triangle. Each socket is 0.025 m. deep for a width of 0.010 m. at the edge, but the central portion is convex and rises to within 0.010 m. of the top surface of the base. In the deep edges remain traces of lead, and in the foremost socket are fragments of bronze, 0.006 m. thick. The circles are distant from each other 0.290–0.296 m.; from center to center they are 0.424–0.430 m. apart. The three bronze objects which the sockets held were backed up immediately against a central support, a marble column, for which a roughened circle, about 0.30 m. in diameter, appears between the three sunken circles; allowing for a smooth anathyrosis of *ca.* 0.03 m., the column must have entirely filled the space between the three sockets, with a diameter of 0.360 m. The column was almost exactly centered on the block. The three sockets, on the other hand, bear a very peculiar relation to the rectangular base; their posi-

---

[64] See above, footnote 40, p. 27.
[65] This base was discovered by Bohn in 1880.

tions were determined by revolving the triangular composition of the sockets around the central column until, on the right side and on the front, the projection of the base beyond the sockets was approximately equal, *ca.* 0.055 m. With this rotation of the sockets, the superposed construction on the base faced in a westerly direction with no regard to the orientation of the neighboring structures. The angle it formed with the steps was approximately $52^1/_2°$ so that it could be viewed frontally by the populace which approached it when passing in front of the steps on the way to the entrance of the Akropolis.

The restoration of this object, and its purpose, are two connected problems. Superficially, at any rate, it resembles an ordinary tripod base, and as such it has generally been interpreted.[66] Its prominent location, however, and the fact that it later actually determined the position of the Propylon, are evidence of its special importance and imply that it had some religious significance. Very unusual are the circular sockets, where we should expect to find for a tripod either shallow depressions with the outlines of lion paws, with or without rectangular dowel holes,[67] or merely rectangular dowel holes.[68] Even more significant is the manner in which the cuttings for the three feet are tangent to the central support, instead of standing free as in all other bronze tripods with central columns. There do exist, however, two other possibilities for the object which stood on this base, other than a tripod.

On account of the peculiarities in the plan of the base, Petersen argued not only that this could not have been for an ordinary tripod, but also that in plan it resembled rather the shape required for a Hekataion standing before the gate.[69] Since we know that such a Hekataion was carved by Alkamenes and set up just to the right of the Mnesiklean Propylaia,[70] probably immediately after the period 437–432 B.C., it is possible that in this base we have the remains of its predecessor, just to the right of the Propylon.[71] In the same way, the Hermes Propylaios, of which an image carved by Alkamenes was set up at the left side of the entrance to the Mnesiklean Propylaia, possibly replaced a Hermes at the left side of the Propylon, symmetrical with the Hekataion.

As for the development of Hekataia, the extant images of Hekate may be divided into three classes: (A) those showing the single form, (B) the triple-headed herms, and (C) the triple-bodied type. The last, although it would be suitable for the cuttings on the base, was apparently the type invented by Alkamenes, according to Pausanias, and so is too recent in date. The two others reach back to an earlier period, but it must be admitted that neither would satisfy the requirements of the base. There is, however, a sub-variety of the second type (Ba), representing three maidens dancing around a triple-headed herm, as in examples at Athens,[72] Samos,[73] Prague,[74] Venice,[75] Paris,[76] and Rome.[77] This type of Hekataion would fit perfectly the traces on the base at the

---

[66] Bohn, 1882, p. 17a; Fabricius, 1886, pp. 187–188; Guillon, 1943, II, pp. 48, 58; Raubitschek, 1949, p. 343.

[67] *IG* I², 770 (Reisch, 1890, p. 75); base from Pythion (Reisch, 1890, p. 81); Amandry, 1976, pp. 56–58, and in general.

[68] Akanthos column at Delphi (T. Homolle, "Monuments figurés de Delphes," *BCH* 32, 1908, p. 231); Monument of Lysikrates (Reisch, 1890, p. 78); *IG* II², 3093 (Reisch, 1890, p. 78, note 1); *IG* II², 3081 (Fabricius, 1886, p. 188); Monument of the Eponymous Heroes (Shear, 1970, p. 164); others in the Theater of Dionysos and the court of the Epigraphical Museum in Athens.

[69] Petersen, 1908a, pp. 49, 91, and 1908b, pp. 29–32. See also Amandry, 1976, pp. 87–91. For Hekataia in general, see Kraus, 1960, and E. Harrison, 1965, pp. 86–98.

[70] Pausanias, II.30.2.

[71] The following discussion, in which it is proposed that the base supported a Hekataion, rather than a tripod, is a condensed, but virtually unchanged version of an unpublished manuscript written by Dinsmoor in 1910 and, obviously, influenced strongly by Petersen.

[72] Petersen, 1881, pp. 24–39, no. Wa; Friederichs and Wolters, 1885, no. 1537; Reinach, 1897, p. 323, no. 8.

[73] T. Wiegand, "Antike Sculpturen in Samos," *AthMitt* 25, 1900, pp. 173–174.

[74] Petersen, 1881, no. Wb, and 1880, pl. IV; Harrison and Verrall, 1890, p. 379; Harrison, 1899, p. 51, fig. 3743; Petersen, 1908b, p. 24, and 1908a, p. 91. This statue is now in Vienna; see Kraus, 1960, p. 129, pls. 7, 8.

[75] Petersen, 1881, no. Wc; Reinach, 1897, p. 322, no. 7.

[76] Petersen, 1881, no. Xa; Reinach, 1888, pl. 112:3, pp. 104–105.

[77] Petersen, 1881, no. Xf.

Propylon. It is suitable, moreover, in signification, since the three bronze dancing maidens would presumably be identified with the Charites, who were worshipped in this very spot in connection with Artemis-Hekate. It could represent a stage of development earlier than the triple-bodied Hekate of Alkamenes, but the proof is lacking since the only Hekataia which we possess "all seem to be late Hellenistic or Roman."[78]

A noteworthy characteristic of these Hekataia is the fact that the central pillar almost always rises above the three heads, not only in the triple-bodied type invented by Alkamenes, but also in the type of the triple herm.[79] In an example in which the column does not so rise, the tops of the three heads are carefully flattened.[80] The central column therefore played an important part in the ritual: these leveled tops of the overtowering columns were evidently destined to receive offerings of food, probably in movable receptacles or dishes.[81]

We might, therefore, restore a Hekataion resembling that at Prague (now at Vienna). The column outside the Propylon was 0.360 m. in diameter; the triangular pier at Prague would be circumscribed around a circle of 0.064 m. diameter, or inscribed in a circle of 0.088 m. diameter,[82] averaging 0.076 m., or about one fifth of the scale of the monument outside the Propylon. This scale of 1:5 agrees also with the maximum radius of the base, 0.080 m. at Prague, 0.367 m. at the Propylon.[83] So the height of the Charites, 0.23 m. at Prague, would be about 1.15 m. at Athens.[84]

A second, and quite possibly a more likely, candidate which I should like to propose here for the object which was supported by the base is a perirrhanterion, or holy-water basin. Such a basin must have stood near the entrance to the Akropolis, and fragments of many perirrhanteria have been found on the site.[85] As similarly proposed for the hypothetical Hekataion, the perirrhanterion would have been supported by a central marble pedestal surrounded by three bronze figures. Parallels of a sort do exist. Broneer's basin from the Archaic temple of Poseidon at Isthmia, although considerably earlier (mid-7th century), was supported by four korai.[86] Raubitschek has published a circular base (no. 378 = E.M. 6326) which contained six circular cuttings regularly spaced along the circumference.[87] These cuttings have about the same depth as ours (0.015 m.) and are located 0.055 m. from their centers to the outer edge of the base (ours are 0.055 m. from the outer edge of the circular cuttings to the outer edge of the base). The assumption is that Raubitschek's pillar, which dates only slightly later than our base (after 480 B.C.), carried a vessel which was supported by six small statues. As for the basin itself, the maximum diameter which ours could have had in front of the Propylon would have been *ca.* 0.75 m., limited by the marble metopes behind it. Whereas earlier perirrhanteria might be larger (Broneer's is 1.235 m.), many of

---

[78] E. Harrison, 1965, p. 95.

[79] Of the examples listed by Petersen (1881, pp. 24–39), the overtowering column appears in his Va (Reinach, 1888, pl. 112:2), Vc, Ve, Vf (Smith, 1900, no. 1343), Vg, Vk, Vn (Reinach, 1888, pl. 32:1–2; Friederichs and Wolters, 1885, no. 1536), Wa, Wc, and Xa. The pieces Vd, Vh, Vi, Vl, Vm, Wb, and Xf are uncertain.

[80] *Katalog der Sammlung antiker Skulpturen* (*Staatliche Museen zu Berlin*) IV, 1931, no. K174, pl. 65, p. 37; Petersen, 1881, no. Vb.

[81] Dinsmoor noted: "I cannot accept the theory suggested by Petersen (1881, pp. 36–37), and later urged with greater insistance by him (1908b, pp. 21–32, and 1908a, pp. 95–96; cf. Sitte, 1910, p. 88), that the central pillar represents Hecate herself, and that the three figures of the type of Alcamenes represent merely the followers or servants of Hecate. It is an attempt to trace pillar worship in a purely utilitarian object. If we accepted Petersen's theory, it would be necessary to assume, in certain monuments of class Ca, a triple stratification: a central column representing Hecate, surrounded by three maidens who, on merging into the form of Hecate, were surrounded by three additional maidens."

[82] Petersen (1881, p. 27) gives the dimensions as 0.065 m. for the broad sides and 0.023 m. for the truncated corners of the pier.

[83] I.e., 0.180 m. (the column) + 0.134 m. (the bronze figure) + 0.053 m. (projection of the base) = 0.367 m.

[84] Petersen estimated about 0.60 m. (1908b, p. 28).

[85] Raubitschek, 1949, pp. 370–413.

[86] Broneer, 1958, pp. 24–27, pls. 10:a, b; 11:a.

[87] Raubitschek, 1949, pp. 372, 406.

those of 530–480 B.C. were about the same size as our possible one.[88] Therefore, although there is no exact parallel for a perirrhanterion such as the one proposed here with bronze figures around a central marble pillar, the idea that a holy-water basin rested on our prominently located base in front of the Propylon cannot be discarded.

[88] Raubitschek, 1949, p. 370, lists for his 1st, 2nd, and 3rd groups: 10 at 0.65 to 0.72 m., 8 at 0.80 to 0.85 m., 4 at 0.90 to 0.95 m., and 7 at 1.10 to 1.20 m.

IV

THE PROPYLON

THE FIRST STAGE: THE KREPIDOMA

The initial phase of construction of the Archaic gate building, which was to replace the simple, ancient entrance, consisted merely of a stylobate and two lower steps of Pentelic marble, which rested partly on bedrock but primarily on poros foundations. The middle step was built snugly against the earlier "tripod base" in area II.[1] At its preserved southern end, this krepidoma was cut with a diagonal joint of 58° 30′ to fit tightly against the pre-existing marble lining of the lower part of the Pelasgian wall, and thus has an orientation of 36° 28′ west of true north. The diagonally cut ends of the stylobate and of the upper part of the poros foundation (backer course of the middle step) below it, both of which abutted the marble metopes, were treated with anathyrosis at this juncture (Pls. 12, 18:b).[2] The conclusion is inescapable that the metope (1.006 m. wide) which still exists in cut-down form at the southern edge of the stylobate (Pls. 18:b, 23:b), and also the next one to the east (now missing), were still standing during this phase of the construction. The only possible explanation for this strange angle, rather than one of 90° which one would expect in a normal building, is that, after work had begun, the plans for the new gate building were temporarily aborted when it was decided not to demolish the interfering Pelasgian wall and its attendant marble lining. As a result, the ends of the new steps had to be adapted with their acute angle. It is inconceivable that the entire Propylon had not been planned at this time, however, since the steps are not those of a free-standing variety, erected merely to solve conveniently a change in outdoor levels, but are most definitely those of a krepidoma, belonging to a building (Pls. 4:b, 21:b): the depth of the top step (1.175 m.) makes sense only for its employment as a column-bearing stylobate. We can but guess at the reason for this temporary cessation of the project. It may well be that some Athenian faction opposed the dismantling of the early fortification wall on grounds of defense. Whatever the reason, there must have been a short period when

---

[1] It had been suggested that these steps were inserted later, when the Propylon was repaired after the Persian invasion; the only ground for this theory is that they show no trace of damage from fire (Köster, 1909, p. 29, note 2). The stylobate and steps, however, were protected from burning timbers falling on them by the masonry superstructure above, and the flames from fallen timbers within the building were directed upward, not horizontally outward. An exact parallel to this situation exists in the Middle Stoa of the Athenian Agora. The fire that destroyed that building was so intense that the inner face of every architectural member is terribly mutilated, yet, at the east end of the structure where the stylobate, steps, and lower drums of the columns are preserved *in situ*, although fire damage on the back of the drums reaches down to within 0.20 m. of the stylobate, the steps and the stylobate itself are fresh and untouched by fire.

[2] On the stylobate, the top band of anathyrosis is 0.075 m. wide and the vertical band is 0.07 m. wide. The band at the top edge of the poros block of the foundation is 0.05 m. wide.

the stair existed by itself, forming an awkward juncture at its southern end with the unaltered marble dado which ran obliquely both to the east and to the west of it.

The krepidoma, which later supported the west, or entrance façade of the Propylon, now exists only in the angle between the Central Building and the Southwest Wing of the Mnesiklean Propylaia (area II).[3] The maximum length preserved of this structure, as measured on the middle step, is 3.50 m. to the point where it was cut away diagonally to give space for the Periklean building, while the maximum length preserved of the stylobate is 3.01 m. (Pl. 9). At the extreme south end, the two lower steps rest on solid bedrock which was cut in step form to receive them; but as the rock descends toward the north, poros foundations intervened. These poros foundations presumably still continue northward beneath the wall and interior marble pavement of the present Propylaia. The stylobate rested in its entirety upon poros foundations.

The three marble steps are composed of blocks 0.420 m., 0.326 m., and 0.318 m. high from bottom to top. The second step, however, is set into a sunken bed 0.006 m. deep on the bottom step, and the stylobate into a bed 0.002 m. deep on the second, while the stylobate itself is partly worked down 0.004 m. at its top. The finished heights of the steps were thus to have been 0.414 m., 0.324 m., and 0.314 m., apparently intended as 1 1/4, 1, and 31/32 D.F. respectively,[4] with the shallowest riser at the top; the total finished height is 1.052 m. (3 7/32 D.F.). The finished level of the stylobate is at 142.808 m. above mean sea level, and thus 0.1085 m. (1/3 D.F.) above the finished level of the marble floor of the later Propylaia at this point.

The sunken bed, 0.052 m. wide, which was dressed down at the back of each tread to the desired finished surface prior to setting the step above it, is an obvious indication that the rest of each tread is unfinished and should eventually have been dressed down to this same level. The risers show the same protective surfaces, but without the characteristic sunken margin dressed down to the finished plane at their bottom edge (Pls. 9, 11:D–D, 21:b). These protective surfaces, both on the risers and treads, are peculiar in that they are treated with smooth drafted borders, about 0.035 m. wide, which frame the exposed planes of each block and enclose a flush, stippled panel; the smooth border at the bottom of the lowest step is wider, about 0.10 m. high. On the treads, however, the border does not return along the back edge, along the finished sunken margin, except on one block, the northern of the two remaining of the bottom step. Like the protective surfaces on the treads, those on the risers were certainly intended to be removed, despite the absence of sunken margins; at each joint, on the risers as well as on the treads, one of each pair of meeting blocks has a beveled edge, leaving an open joint 0.004 m. wide and 0.005 m. deep. Only in the finished margins at the back of the treads do we find perfectly tight joints.[5] Also, the top front edge of each step, and both the front and back edges of the stylobate, at the juncture of riser and tread, are beveled for a width and height of about 0.008 m.; this bevel is somewhat worn away by foot traffic near the termination of the krepidoma at the north, where the blocks were partially cut away at the order of Mnesikles.

The present widths of the bottom and second treads are 0.447 and 0.449 m. (1 3/8 D.F.); identical widths would have appeared on the finished steps if the protective surface of the risers had been dressed off to an estimated depth of 0.005 m. The stylobate is 1.175 m. wide across its present top, so that, if the front and back faces had been dressed off, the finished width would have been about 1.165 m. (3 9/16 D.F.).

---

[3] Only the stylobate had been uncovered in 1840; the second step was apparently discovered in 1880 by Bohn (although he saw only 0.140 m. of its height, 1882, p. 16b), while the bottom step was revealed by Weller in 1901.

[4] The Doric foot (D.F.) had a length of 0.326 to 0.327 m. See Dinsmoor, 1950, notes on pp. 54, 161, 195, 199.

[5] See Hodge, 1975, pp. 333–347, for a discourse on beveled joints cut within the thickness of the protective surface of blocks.

The inner vertical face of the stylobate has rusticated panels identical to those of the outer face, except that they have flush, smooth borders at top and sides only (Pls. 11:C-C, 18:a). The treated surface is 0.17 m. high. Below this is a roughly worked projection which continues to the bottom of the blocks and extends into the building about 0.055 m. The treatment is much like that along the lower part of a normal euthynteria course where the blocks are buried below grade level and do not need to be finished. Our case is similar in that this projection was below the originally planned floor construction with its thickness of 0.146 m. (see p. 40 below).[6]

At the south end of the krepidoma, where the steps were cut obliquely to fit against the pre-existing construction of the forecourt, the southern block of the lowest step, with a length of 1.657 m., was given a short, square-edged corner return, at right angles to its face, for a depth of 0.040 m. Thereafter it is cut off at an angle of 55°08' to fit against a rock step. The southern block of the middle step is 1.770 m. long, with its south end beveled to fit against the marble facing of the Pelasgian wall. The southern block of the stylobate, with a length of 1.789 m., was cut, as was the lower step, with a short, square-edged corner return, at right angles to its face (including here the usual 0.005 m. bevel), for a depth of 0.012 m.; from this point backward it is cut obliquely at an angle of 58°30', with anathyrosis, for the full width of the block, and thereby the length at the back of the stylobate block is reduced to 1.073 m.[7]

A single intermediate joint remains in each step; these joints show no regularity of arrangement. Measuring from the joint of the middle step, the joint in the stylobate is 0.388 m. to the north and that of the bottom step is 0.862 m., also to the north (Pl. 9). Instead of coinciding, these upper and lower joints differ by 0.474 m. The jointing system, therefore, was apparently quite random and thus gives no clue to the intended column spacing.

In the present condition of the krepidoma, the north end of each of the steps is roughly cut off in the same plane, at an angle of 65°43' to the face; in fact, the entire Propylon was truncated at this same angle to permit the construction of the south toichobate of the Central Building of the Mnesiklean Propylaia, though diverging from the proper orientation by 00°20'. This diagonally cut end of the krepidoma lies only 0.065/0.075 m. from the outer face of the Mnesiklean marble toichobate, as a result of which the uppermost poros foundation course of the Propylaia overlaps the second step by about 0.07 m., while the next course of the foundation, projecting 0.495 m. from the toichobate, is undercut about 0.435 m. to respect the diagonally cut end of the lowest marble step. In other words, when the Propylon was first cut through, Mnesikles did not make proper allowance for the projecting foundations of his Propylaia; then, during construction of the Propylaia, instead of hewing off more of the hard marble blocks of the Propylon, he preferred to trim the softer poros of the new work. As a result of the adjustment to the Mnesiklean building, only two blocks remain in each step of the early krepidoma; each block is cut off obliquely at one end, the south ends being original and the north ends retrimmed in 437 B.C.

As for the construction, the joints have remained so tightly closed that it is impossible to ascertain with complete certainty in which direction the work proceeded or how the blocks were doweled and clamped;[8] if they were visible, we should probably see double-T clamps. The blocks

---

[6] Weller states that the projecting lower part of this inner face is a ledge designed to support floor slabs, but this seems contrary to normal practice. The marble paving slab on which Weller restored his complete marble pavement floor (1904, pp. 36–37, 41–42, 55, pl. I) was not an original part of the building.

[7] Bohn represents it as mitered at 45°, without connection with the bevel at the front (1882, pl. III); Weller shows it correctly (1904, pl. II).

[8] From the chamfer at the south end of each of the two extant stylobate blocks (i.e., the north side of each contact joint), this course, according to the findings of Hodge (1975, pp. 333–347) for other buildings, should have been pried in a northerly direction. This would accord with the southernmost trapezoidal block of the stylobate being the last laid, dropped into place after being carefully cut to fit against the yet standing, earlier metopes, during the temporary interruption in the construction of the Propylon.

were set in place by means of tongs and lifting bosses, which projected from the front and back of each stone, at the gravitational center. All the bosses on the faces of the steps were afterwards hewn off, except that on the southern block of the lowest step (Pls. 11, 21:b).[9]

THE SECOND STAGE: THE ORIGINAL PROPYLON

The initial phase of the Propylon was quite simple to carry out, since it appears to have consisted merely of erecting the stylobate and steps of the krepidoma. The second stage, the actual construction of the gate building, was a much more extensive project. During this period, the early gateway and that part of the massive Pelasgian wall which interfered with the new construction were removed. The northern extension of the lining of marble metopes also disappeared; remnants of only the two southernmost of these interfering slabs remained, the one at the south-west corner of the stylobate, which was now cut down in height, and two fragments of the next one to the north, which were found in 1975 in the bedrock cutting which originally held the entire metope. The bedrock in the area of the Propylon where the Pelasgian wall had stood was leveled off 0.146 m. below the finished stylobate (0.150 m. below the level of the protective surface), and bedrock in the other areas which have been exposed, III and IV in the Central Building of the Propylaia, was also leveled to create solid bearing for floor slabs and step blocks. On the leveled bedrock in the southwest corner of the building was placed the southern wall of the Propylon. The lower part of the wall consists of marble blocks, two courses in height, surmounted by a single row of marble orthostates and, above that, a marble string course; the two lower courses of blocks projected inwards from the plane of the orthostates, in a seat-like arrangement. At this same time the top, horizontal plane at the southern end of the stylobate was dressed down 0.004 m., removing the protective surface in the area where the parastas was to be placed (Pls. 9, 21:a, 22:a). The trapezoidal marble filler block which closed the outer face of this anta wall against the Pelasgian wall was erected (Pls. 4:c, 11:D-D, 21:b), and certainly the anta and the remainder of the anta wall were also set in place, although this material has now disappeared. Presumably the north wall and east stylobate of the building were erected as well, but the evidence is lacking and it is impossible to know to what degree this Propylon of the 480's (see p. 54 below) was finished.

I shall first describe the cuttings in, or levelings of, the bedrock, and afterwards attempt to interpret them.

FLOOR AND STEP CUTTINGS

In area II, within the southwest corner of the Propylon, we have already mentioned that the rock was worked down to an average level of 0.146 m. below that of the finished stylobate, i.e. to 142.662 m. above mean sea level. The picked surface is remarkably even, varying only 0.002 m. from the norm. This surface was obviously prepared to receive the blocks of the south wall, but it extends, to where it is now broken away, another 0.06 m. further into the building than did the marble platform blocks on which the orthostates of the wall rested, and so must have borne some relationship to the flooring of the building (Pls. 9, 11:B-B).

In area III, within the central passage of the Mnesiklean structure, there exist horizontally cut planes separated by vertical steps, which run parallel to the extended west stylobate of the

---

[9] This boss was discovered by Weller (1904, p. 41).

Propylon (Plan A). The lines of the risers are somewhat rough, but lie *ca.* 10.58 m., 11.60 m., and 13.30 m. east of the outer edge of the stylobate. The top riser is now visible for a length of 2.65 m., from 6.15 m. to 8.80 m. north of the extended face of the southern flank wall (measured from the bottom of the sloping orthostate); it is interrupted by a channel which was later cut along the middle of the Mnesiklean structure. East of this line, for a short distance, the rock seems to have been recut at a later date: the bed slopes up from 143.45 m. to 143.546–143.587 m. above sea level (Pl. 14). Further east the rock is horizontal, at elevation + 143.865 m., only 0.145 m. below the adjacent Mnesiklean floor, and continues eastward at this level to the east stylobate of the later Propylaia before it rises again; no earlier cuttings east of the top riser can be discerned. To the west of this riser, however, the bedrock is cut horizontally for a width of 1.70 m., at elevation + 143.280 m., its boundaries being oriented with reference to the Propylon; the west edge can be traced for a length of 3.55 m., from 6.48 m. to 10.03 m. north of the extended face of the southern flank wall. The only irregularity in the ledge, which occurs at a point 9.50 m. from the southern flank wall, is a drop of 0.02 m. which indicates merely a difference in dressing the beds for super-posed blocks of varying heights. West of this shelf, in turn, is a step which varies from 0.82 to 1.20 m. in width. In this strip we find elevations varying from 142.835 m. to 142.930 m. and 142.970 m. To the west of this step is a lower surface, which has no proper western edge. Its elevation is 142.700–142.708 m., which is only *ca.* 0.042 m. higher than that of the cut bedrock in the southwest corner of the Propylon, and therefore seems to indicate the basic level to which the rock was worked to support the floor in the western part of the Propylon (Pl. 14).

We now turn to area IV, in the north aisle of the Central Building of the Propylaia. Here, in the central part of the cleared area, there is a worked ledge with a maximum width of 1.05 m., with an anomalous west edge, but with an east riser, the line of which closely parallels the steps and the Archaic gatehouse proper. Its elevation is 142.23 m. above sea level, and so some 0.43 m. below the other lowest worked surfaces within the Propylon (Pl. 7). The riser, which lies 9.22 m. east of the outer edge of the projected west stylobate, has only a short preserved length of 0.72 m., from 15.40 to 16.12 m. north of the extended face of the southern flank wall. The upper ledge to the east of the riser, at elevation + 142.395 m., was evidently cut down at the order of Mnesikles in preparation for the floor of the Propylaia;[10] presumably its original elevation was *ca.* 142.700 m., which conflicted with Mnesikles' finished floor of that same elevation and necessitated the cutting down of 0.305 m. of bedrock to allow for the later paving slabs.[11]

In area IV, since the level of the central bedrock ledge bears no relation to the levels which were prepared by Mnesikles for his structure, and, indeed, forced him to adopt here a very thin subfloor construction of trapezoidal blocks, we can be confident that the surface of this ledge was

---

[10] This elevation accords closely to that of the top of the poros subflooring blocks which were installed by Mnesikles and upon which rested his marble paving slabs which, including their protective surface of 0.01 m., had thicknesses here of 0.314, 0.315, 0.323, 0.334, and 0.349 m.

[11] See Bundgaard, 1957, pp. 30–44, and 1976, p. 154. Bundgaard used the incorrect Kavvadias-Kawerau system of sea-level readings, and has slight differences in elevations in his own two publications:

		Bundgaard 1957	Bundgaard 1976	Dinsmoor	Difference
Area II	Stylobate	+ 143.38	+ 143.29	+ 142.808	.482/.572
	Later paving block	143.29	–	142.736	.554
	Bedrock under floor	–	–	142.662	–
Area III	Rock under floor at east	144.47	144.47	143.865	.605
	Rock under gate	143.85	143.87	143.280	.570/.590
	Rock under step to west	143.50	–	142.930	.570
	Rock under floor to west	143.27	143.00?	142.708	.562
Area IV	Rock cutting	142.79	–	142.230	.560

prepared for a pre-existing structure.[12] Since the eastern step-up from the ledge parallels the remaining portions of the Propylon, we must assume it was prepared for that building and that the ledge was within the confines of the Propylon. Since the level of this ledge is respectively 0.432 m. and 0.478 m. lower than those of the bedrock at the southwest corner of the building in area II and in front of the rock-cut steps in area III, it must have been cut at a location where the naturally sloping bedrock failed to meet requirements and had to be cut down deeper to form a level surface for a sub-floor construction.

Because of this large cut-down patch in the bedrock in area IV, and of the undoubtedly many other patches and the resulting built-up floor construction that would have been necessary, especially in the northwestern part of the building where the rock slopes off to the west, it seems impossible to believe that the entire mismatched surface of the floor area, of creviced bedrock and poros fillers at elevation + 142.662-142.708 m., was not planned to be covered with floor slabs comparable in workmanship and material to the enframing monumental marble building, the quality of which is represented by its beautifully worked krepidoma and southern wall; the design of the gate building cannot be compared to that of the patchy rock-cut steps of the earlier forecourt. Similar reasoning forces one to restore finished steps over the roughly cut, uneven rock-cut steps in area III, especially since there are ledges of slightly differing elevation cut on these rock steps, indicating the reception of blocks of varying heights (Pl. 14).[13] Let us now return to area II, just inside the western stylobate. Here there is a marble block, re-used at a later period as a paving slab, and now tilted slightly out of place, with its top variously 0.072 to 0.082 m. below the finished stylobate (see p. 55 below). It cannot be considered as part of the original construction, although Weller and Bundgaard tried to identify it as such (see footnote 13 above). There exists also in this area part of the original leveled bedrock within the building. This bedrock, which lies 0.146 m. below the finished stylobate, is only 0.046 m. lower than the dressed bedrock just west of the rock-cut steps in area III. We have already made a case against bedrock (with scattered fillers) as having been the material for the originally designed flooring, and, in any event, such a step-down of 0.146 m., from the stylobate into the building, would have been an unnecessary hazard. One is left with the alternative, and the one which is the most normal, of a planned interior floor of marble slabs, 0.146 m. thick, which would have finished flush with the stylobate. The probability is that this flooring was never installed in the original, unfinished building, inasmuch as the back of the stylobate has no anathyrosis but retains a flush, stippled panel treatment. One may object that if the floor were planned, anathyrosis would have been applied to the back of the stylobate blocks before they were laid. The stylobate, however, was laid in an earlier phase, prior to the construction of the Propylon, and a form of anathyrosis could always be cut at a later date, during building operations; this is exactly what happened at the back of the stylobate blocks of the Hephaisteion and of the temple of Poseidon at Sounion where again the vertical surface was treated with stippled paneling and flush borders prior to receiving a smooth upper edge and a hacked-down,

[12] The two poros sub-flooring blocks south of center, on the west side of the cleared area, have a narrow ledge at the same level as that of the original bedrock surface of the Propylon just to the east; thin trapezoidal poros fillers, 0.165 m. thick, must have rested on this narrow ledge and on the earlier bedrock cutting of the Propylon in order to support the Mnesiklean paving slabs in this area (Pl. 7).

[13] Weller (1904) considered the re-used marble block that is of the post-Persian remodeling and that lies, moved slightly out of place, near the southwest corner of the building as being original, and repeated the dimensions of this block, as a module, to pave the entire floor (*ibid.*, pl. 1); he recognized a difficulty at the rock-cut steps to the east. He says (*ibid.*, p. 55) that the marble slab is 0.03 m. lower than the rock floor at the foot of the steps (in actuality, the sloping top of the slab averages 0.023 m. higher than the rock floor at the foot of the steps, and was originally 0.028 m. higher). Bundgaard (1957, fig. 22, p. 32) also uses this later slab as original, calling it "*in situ*". At the rock-cut steps, he uses the bedrock as the floor, but ignores what happened in between. In Bundgaard, 1976, p. 154, he shows a mixture of materials for the steps, some of bedrock and others of a nameless material; his figure 89 is sketchy and does not, in actuality, conform to the planes of the cuttings for the steps which still exist (see Pl. 14).

recessed surface below that to create anathyrosis after the blocks had been set in place. The fact that a marble floor was contemplated, sloping down 0.046 m. from the stair at the east to the west front for drainage, seems inescapable (Pl. 14). We shall never know if any of the final flooring was actually laid in place, since the early floor, being higher than the Mnesiklean, would necessarily have been removed, but because of the lack of anathyrosis of the stylobate and the fact that in the post-Persian period a totally new, incongruous floor was constructed, 0.072 m. lower than the finished stylobate, it seems likely that the work, if started, was never completed, especially at the southwest corner of the building. The possibility that the finished steps were placed in position is stronger, since the slightly varying levels which appear on the rock-cut steps were provided for upper blocks of different heights, and such work was not done unless the actual blocks were on hand.

THE FLANK WALL

The south flank wall in area II, at right angles to the stylobate of the façade, cuts through the Pelasgian wall at an angle of 33°43'. Its present maximum height, to the top of the poros backing at the west end, is 3.050 m. (Pls. 10, 11:C–C). The maximum preserved length is about 5.10 m. from the beveled corner which marks the inner face of the original parastas to the end of the easternmost poros backer block that is still extant; the flank wall is then hewn off, like the krepidoma, to give place to the Mnesiklean structure.[14]

The finished, inner face of the side wall reaches a height of 1.919 m. above the dressed bedrock sub-floor level. This wall is composed of four marble courses, two narrow ones at the bottom, an orthostate course, and a thin string course (Pls. 10, 11, 20:a, 21:a).

The first course, 0.380 m. high, or 0.234 m. higher than the finished floor, rests on solid rock, and, as indicated by the westernmost block of the series, which is now cut down to the post-Persian floor level, projected forward 0.640 m. from the line of the bottom of the orthostates, or third course, in the form of a step. The original vertical face of this step course which is preserved only partially at the southwest corner, 0.85 m. long and 0.074 m. high, is treated with a stippled surface. This first block at the west was 1.842 m. in length, overlapping the stylobate by 0.150 m.[15] The second block of this course is 1.271 m. long, and the third, cut off at an angle to give place for the Mnesiklean Propylaia (Pls. 3:a, 4:a, b), has a maximum preserved length of about 1.40 m.; both of these last two blocks evidently had the same original projection of 0.640 m., although they are now so mutilated that the evidence is lacking.

The second course also projected forward in the form of a platform, or seat, resting on the lower step. The height of this course is 0.272 m.; the exact amount of the projection is unknown, for the blocks were later cut back to the plane of the orthostates above them. The fact that they originally projected forward, however, is proved both by the very rough picking of their present faces and by the gaping joints between their ends where the anathyroses, which once closed the joints at the

---

[14] Before the character of this construction was recognized, Hoffer's plan (Schöll, 1841, p. 116, note, pl. CCCXC: fig. 3) showed the wall and stylobate as meeting at an acute angle, and that of Chaudet (1852, pl. 193), at an obtuse angle. Beulé wrongly assumed that the Pelasgian wall curved at this point, the south wall of the Propylon then becoming a mere facing applied outside the Pelasgian wall (Beulé, 1862, p. 43).

[15] Its western end is badly broken, but assuredly aligned with the preserved end of the next course above. As a result, it was notched vertically for 0.146 m. at its bottom where it was cut to rest partially on the stylobate. An incised setting line on the stylobate, 0.659 m. outside the line of the bottom of the orthostate, was perhaps intended for this block; two other setting lines, 0.092 m. and 0.298 m. south of the first one, also appear on the stylobate. A pressure line, 0.147 m. back from, and parallel to, the edge of the stylobate, was probably caused by this step block as well. The marble metope which lay back of the southeastern corner of the stylobate, and which created spatial conflict with this block, was now necessarily removed.

original face, have been hewn away. It is possible that the top of this second projecting course served as a platform for the display of trophies and dedications, in which case it may have extended out from the wall above about as far as did the course below it. Since, however, the height of this second course (0.272 m.) agrees closely with that of the benches in the forecourt (0.292 m.) and with that of the benches into which the lower course within the Propylon was cut at a later period (0.255 m.), we have suggested here that this second course represented a bench, as is often found lining the inner walls of gatehouses.[16] We may then, perhaps, restore the original projection as having been *ca.* 0.357 m. like those of the benches in the forecourt and the later ones in the Propylon, which evidently replaced these earlier ones (Pl. 17).[17] Of this original seat course, three blocks remain in position: the westernmost, 1.610 m. long, has its west end 0.012 m. from the original parastas, as did the course below (Pl. 4:C); the second is 1.732 m. long; and the third is hewn off for the later Propylaia, with a maximum preserved length of 1.21 m. (Pls. 10, 19:a, 20:a). The westernmost block of both the step and seat courses overlay the diagonal cutting at the south end of the stylobate and, along with the original parastas, hid this earlier, awkward cutting from view (Pls. 4:c, 18:a).

The third course is composed of orthostates 1.182 m. in height. The orthostates have a forward inclination, toward the interior of the building, amounting to 0.045 m. in their total height,[18] giving a rate of 0.038 m. per meter of height. Only two blocks of this course remain. The one which adjoins the parastas has a finished length of 1.282 m. (bottom) and 1.284 m. (top), but its actual length is considerably more, of which only another 0.181 m. (bottom) and 0.171 m. (top) can now be seen before the block disappears behind the later poros parastas.[19] The maximum preserved length of the second block is 3.33 m., but its east end has been hewn off to make way for the later Propylaia.[20] Near the present right end of the first block exists the preparation for the abutting of the original anta wall in the form of a vertical joint surface (revealed by the later alterations). This consists, first, of a bevel, 0.005 m. wide and 0.009 m. deep (Pl. 13), indicating that the inner face of the original parastas was 0.162 m. from the east edge of the stylobate, and that it was vertical.[21] West of the bevel, which was merely the joint between the protective surfaces, appears the true joint between the marble orthostate and the original anta wall, a smooth anathyrosis, 0.051 m. wide, which inclines inwards horizontally on a slight slope to as much as 0.006 m. from the inner edge of the bevel (0.015 m. from the outer face of the orthostate). West of that is a roughly sunken surface which seems to have been partially reworked during the later rebuilding at the re-entrant corner where the poros anta wall abuts it (Pl. 13). This sunken surface is now set back 0.037 m. at the bottom to 0.057 m. at the top from the outer face of the orthostate.

The back of the eastern orthostate is very rough and irregular; its thickness varies from 0.24 to 0.47 m. The western one is more uniform, *ca.* 0.295 m. thick. Their faces are treated very similarly

---

[16] Two projecting courses of this form, the lower a step and the upper a seat, are found in the Propylon at Gaggera (Selinous); usually there was only one course, the step being omitted, as in the Mnesiklean Propylaia. Such seats provided a resting place for those who arrived before the gates were opened.

[17] In Weller's restoration these conditions are overlooked, and the present seat is treated as if it were original.

[18] This is measured at the edge nearest the parastas, to avoid the results of displacement.

[19] I could measure at least 0.058 m. further in, behind the poros blocks, proving that over all the blocks is more than 1.521 m. long.

[20] It has been suggested verbally that, because of its unusual length, this second block may be re-used from the epistyle of an earlier building, which must, then, have been of about the scale of the old Athena temple. The material alone should disqualify this idea, since an all-marble building, already destroyed by the mid-480's, seems unlikely. It also is hard to conceive how such a block, when such an expanse of good surface could be salvaged for its exposed face, would have so limited a preserved depth, of only 0.24 to 0.47 m., and such a rough back.

[21] The present poros parastas leans eastward 0.008 m. in the height of the orthostate.

to those of the steps of the krepidoma, with a smooth border 0.035-0.045 m. wide around all four edges, and with the central panel stippled, but in the same plane as the borders.[22] This again, as for the steps, is obviously a protective surface, indicating that the structure was unfinished.[23] The orthostates offer the most convincing evidence that the structure is pre-Persian; their calcined and cracked surfaces can only be the result of fire. In workmanship they show another primitive detail: at the re-entrant corner made with the original parastas the protective surface of the orthostate was mitered contiguous with the protective surface of the parastas; in more developed work the miters of the protective surfaces would have been spread apart to form vertical sunken margins at the corner, the perpendicular surfaces of which would have been at the desired finished plane of the walls. A similar treatment of vertical interior angles, but in poros construction, appears at the re-entrant corner of the steps of the forecourt, below the Pelasgian wall. This method of treating a vertical interior angle corresponds to the similar treatment of the horizontal interior angles on the risers of the krepidoma (see p. 36 above). From the depth of the bevel we learn that the surface to be removed from the orthostates was 0.009 m. thick. No clamps were used for the construction of the orthostate course, nor, so far as is now determinable, for the two lower courses on which they rested.

A few incised lines appear on the marble orthostates, but they seem to lack any significant meaning. Three of them are horizontal, appearing at distances of 0.537 m., 0.591 m., and 0.635 m. below the top of the course. Two other lines rise slightly (about 0.02 m. per meter of length) from west to east; where they cross the extant joint, they are 0.310 m. and 0.970 m. below the top of the orthostates. One vertical line appears at a distance of 1.775 m. east of the joint between the two extant blocks.

Of more importance is a series of nail holes in the marble orthostates.[24] Seventeen of these sporadically placed holes are now preserved, the highest being exactly at the top joint of the course, the lowest 0.57 m. below the top (Pl. 10). Eight holes are 0.007 m. in diameter and 0.01-0.015 m. deep. Three others (of the same diameter) are barely incised, and two of these were apparently markers for the uppermost of the sloping incised lines. Five are 0.01 m. in diameter and 0.01-0.03 m. deep. The single hole in the top joint is 0.007 m. in diameter and 0.055 m. deep, and contains part of a rusted iron nail. Apparently most of these holes contained nails or hooks supporting temporary decorations (garlands or fillets) and they seem to be post-Persian in date.[25]

It has always been recognized that the three lower marble courses of the flank wall were built together with a backing of poros blocks.[26] These poros blocks are roughly worked on all faces and are somewhat loosely set together, without clamps. The top of the extant blocks back of the marble orthostates are level with, or closely level with, the top of these orthostates; in this course

---

[22] Judeich (1931, p. 226) erroneously speaks of these blocks as metopes of the old Hekatompedon.

[23] Ross assumed that these blocks, like the later anta, were roughened in order to receive stucco (Ross, 1855, p. 82; cf. p. 79). Bohn, on the other hand, concluded that this treatment proves that the blocks were not originally to have been stuccoed (Bohn, 1882, p. 16b).

[24] These were noted by Ross (1855, p. 80) and Weller (1904, p. 65, pl. III).

[25] Since these holes are very similar to those on the inner side of the poros anta wall (see p. 61 below), which must date to the 460's (see p. 64 below), I conclude that the two sets were made at about the same time, in the Kimonian period. Ross suggested, partly because of the fact that the wall was burnt, that these nails supported the fetters of the Chalkidians and Boiotians which Herodotos (v.77) saw hanging from walls that the Medes' fire had charred, opposite the megaron (i.e. the opisthodomos of the old Athena temple) facing west. The location, however, is not suitable for the Propylon. The word used by Herodotos, "τειχέων" (τεῖχος), primarily meant, at his time, city wall or fortification (J. E. Powell, *A Lexicon to Herodotus,* Cambridge 1938, p. 352; H. G. Liddell and R. Scott, *A Greek-English Lexicon*), and so might very well refer to the inner side of the Pelasgian wall to the north of the Propylon, a very conspicuous construction and one that faced the opisthodomos of the old Athena temple.

[26] Ross, 1855, p. 79; Burnouf, 1877, p. 186; Bohn, 1882, p. 16; Bötticher, 1888, p. 89; Middleton, 1892, p. 15; Miller, 1893, p. 519; Weller, 1904, pp. 38-39; Kavvadias and Kawerau, 1906, cols. 138-140.

the stones are 0.35–0.52 m. thick and make the overall thickness of the flank wall 0.78–0.83 m. There is no indication that any part of this extant irregular southern outer face was to have been exposed, since it was backed up and hidden for a length of some 10 meters by the Pelasgian wall. Only at its now missing eastern end, where it would have protruded beyond the limits of the early fortification wall, would it have been entirely exposed (Pl. 16).[27]

Next above the orthostates came a string course of marble, 0.085 m. high,[28] flush with the proposed finished face of the orthostate course,[29] and so 0.009 m. behind the stippled surface. Evidently, therefore, this narrow course was perfectly finished. Only a small fragment of the course is now preserved, 0.22 m. in length, at the west end of the flank wall (Pl. 10).[30] It terminated at the west in a joint surface, in line with the back of the bevel in the course below. Whether this band continued around the corner along the face of the original anta wall is conjectural, but perfectly possible. The level at its top is the same as the level at the top of the exterior trapezoidal filler block at the south end of the parastas, and therefore the same as the level at the top of one of the original, replaced marble blocks (the third) of the anta wall (see p. 47 below). The string course could very well have been set into a slot cut part way into the top of the block of the anta wall, just as the later string course in the Pinakotheke was placed. The length of the thin westernmost slab was originally 1.13 m., as we learn from a tooled bed and pry cutting on the orthostate course below; other pry cuttings, a pair 2.40 and 2.44 m. farther east, imply that the intermediate slabs were probably about 1.20 m. in length (Pl. 9).[31]

In construction, this string course is very peculiar, being 0.55 m. deep, whereas the poros backing wall, which is preserved at this point considerably higher than the top of the orthostates, lies only 0.36 m. behind the finished face of the orthostates; for the extra depth of 0.19 m., therefore, a rebate, or mortise, 0.21 m. deep and 0.11 m. high at the front (0.14 m. high at the back), was cut in the face of the poros backer block to house the back part of the string course, and the backing wall and facing were thus loosely bonded together (Pls. 11:C–C, 21:a). The bed of the mortise is 0.012 m. below the top surface of the orthostates; probably the back part of the thin marble slab rested on a clay bed.

The reconstruction of the upper, missing part of the finished wall that rested on this string course is completely hypothetical. Two possibilities exist, that it was made of wood and stucco or, more aesthetically pleasing, that it was continued upward in marble. The former of these possibilities was embraced by Weller and by Dinsmoor, partly on the ground that the thin slabs could not have borne a great weight, partly on the ground that the top surface of the string course has a picked finish and would therefore have been too rough to have allowed a tight joint with superposed blocks, and partly, but most especially, because of the existence of a shallow cutting on the top of this course. I will present this solution first.

The cutting begins 0.18 m. from the west end of the extant slab and 0.082 m. back from its front face. The depression is rectangular, 0.205 m. from front to back but indeterminate as to width since the slab is broken. Its depth is 0.028 m. The sides and bottom of the cutting are somewhat

---

[27] The Pelasgian wall, 5.85 m. thick, intersected at an angle of 56° 17′, would present a surface of 10.54 m.

[28] This was first described by Bohn (1882, p. 16b, pls. VIII, X); cf. Bötticher, 1888, p. 89; Judeich, 1931, p. 226. The most complete description was given by Weller, 1904, p. 39.

[29] This was also noted by Weller; Bohn had represented it as projecting forward from the orthostates.

[30] Bohn drew this course as if a considerable length were preserved; Weller says that he saw only 0.18 m. of it. As Weller noted apropos of his photograph (1904, p. 39, note 1, fig. 2), after his departure from Athens it "evidently suffered some displacement, and is now thrust forward a little." When Dinsmoor first saw it in 1908, only the rear half remained *in situ*; subsequently he found three other pieces and several splinters, and was able to restore the slab as Weller had seen it.

[31] The top of the orthostate is injured at the possible location of the second joint.

rough. It seems difficult to find a reasonable use for such a depression with stone to stone construction, but it might have received a wooden member. Weller suggested a continuous wall of wood above this level of the string course,[32] but such a design seems quite improbable. A more natural solution would have been to build this upper wall of mud brick, covered with stucco and reinforced with periodically placed vertical wooden members. The marble string course would then have formed the base of the stuccoed surface, which would possibly have been covered with wall paintings if the structure had been finished;[33] the whole arrangement would then be strongly reminiscent of the later treatment of the interior of the Pinakotheke, and may, indeed, have given Mnesikles the idea for his design. We can assume that the vertical wooden reinforcing struts were 0.20 m. square, placed in square sockets. We may also assume that the bricks were of the normal size, 0.45 m. square, but cut into halves. The brick filling between the vertical wooden posts would probably have been placed somewhat back from the outer edge of the string course so that the finished stucco would also be slightly recessed from the vertical plane of the wall below. The narrow, horizontal ledge thus created would be necessary to form a break between the disparate materials of the upper and lower walls. Between the brick wall and the poros backing wall, furthermore, there would then have been an air space of several centimeters, its purpose being to prevent the infiltration of moisture from the Pelasgian retaining wall behind.[34]

The preserved higher part of the poros backing wall, above the top of the orthostates, is set, as we noted, 0.36 m. behind the finished marble wall surface. Only one block of this backing now remains, with a thickness of 0.46 m.; the back of it is not finished, although it is cut to an even plane. The west end is vertical, located about 0.05 m. west of the interior corner of the Propylon; the east end is broken away. This poros block is 0.945 m. high (Pls. 11:C–C, 21:a). Next above it comes a poros course only 0.288 m. high, with its front now broken away. It may originally have extended northwards as far as the face of the brick wall below, but no further, since it would be necessary for the stucco finish to pass over it unimpeded. To counterbalance this outward projection, the course protruded 0.10 m. at the back, behind the line of the poros course below it, and thus would have had a maximum depth of about 0.88 m. This, then, would have formed a horizontal reinforcing course for the brick wall, just as the wood struts formed the vertical reinforcement. Such an alternating system for the backing wall would probably have risen to the ceiling level, in pseudo-isodomic form. A system of this sort gives a possible solution for the flank walls above the string course.

The second possibility for the reconstruction of the upper wall is that of continuing it to the ceiling in marble. We must first turn to the earlier objections to this theory. The argument that the string course was too thin to have borne the weight of a marble superstructure can perhaps best be met with the parallel of the string course of the later Pinakotheke which carries a heavy marble wall above it. Although this course is slightly thicker than ours, it is made of brittle Eleusinian limestone. It is true that along its greater length it is inset into the wall for only about one third of the wall thickness, but at the gatewall it appears on both finished sides and occupies almost two thirds of the wall thickness. With either solution, however, it is carrying about the same number of

---

[32] Weller, 1904, p. 39.

[33] Cf. Dörpfeld, 1911b, pp. 87–96. Weller strangely objects to such a treatment because brick "is not employed above marble, and because the thin marble slab would not be needed to support stuccoed courses" (Weller, 1904, p. 39). Many temples, such as the Heraion at Olympia and the temples at Mon Repos (on Corfu) and at Lepreion (west of Bassai), had mud-brick walls above stone orthostates. Although these orthostates were not of marble, it would not be impossible that our building, one of the first to employ local marble from Penteli, was constructed in this fairly common fashion.

[34] A similar expedient appears in the Stoa of Eumenes, where the arches form air spaces separating the stuccoed back wall of the Stoa from the retaining wall of the Asklepieion.

kilograms per square centimeter as ours would be, and, in any case, when under compression and with a solid bearing surface under them, stone slabs have little danger of cracking. The second objection was that the picked surface on top of the string course would not allow a tight joint with superposed marble blocks. Here, one can merely remark that the top surface of the orthostates, on which this self-same marble string course rests, is also quite roughly worked. Lastly, the incomplete cutting on top of the extant thin slab poses more of a problem. It is incomplete, however, and we do not know with any certainty whether it is original or not.

Now let us turn to the post-Persian remodeling of the anta and anta wall at the south end of the stylobate (Pl. 11:D–D). If we accept this as a fairly crude attempt at a somewhat faithful rebuilding of the original structure, as I think one must, we are quite safe in assuming the entire original anta wall to have been composed of marble blocks, from bottom to top (Pl. 15:B′). Then, if we look at the southern end of the poros blocks of the later parastas (Pls. 9, 13), we find that the treatment of the upper two courses, above the level of the orthostates of the flank wall, is just like that of the lower courses which abut the orthostates, i.e. that they have anathyrosis. This indicates that masonry construction may well have been employed above the orthostates and string course of the flank wall in the remodeling work, and that it therefore may just as well have occurred in the original building as well. Such a solution, with masonry to masonry contact for the full height of the interior corner of the Propylon, seems much more fitting than that of plaster abutting marble from the top of the string course to the ceiling.

THE ANTA AND THE ANTA WALL

Little evidence is left for the original form of the parastas of the west façade, but there is certainly more evidence than has previously been recognized. The extant marble anta and poros blocks of the wall behind it, in area II, are from the later remodeling of the Propylon.[35] Of the work done in this first period, we now have only the slightly lowered area on top of the stylobate where the protective surface was removed in preparation for placing the parastas (Pl. 9), the trapezoidal marble filler block at the southwestern corner of the anta wall (Pl. 11:D–D), a ledge cutting on the Pelasgian wall which was used to bond the Propylon and Pelasgian walls together (Pls. 10, 11:C–C), and the working of the vertical joint surface on the western marble orthostate of the flank wall for the reception of the corner wall blocks of the anta wall (Pls. 10, 13).

A large part of the now extant portion of the stylobate has been worked 0.004 m. (varying from 0.003 to 0.006 m.) below the protective surface down to the finished level, to receive a parastas with its anta. This worked-down area begins 0.048–0.051 m. behind the present front face of the stylobate and extends to the rear edge; it covers the entire southern block and reaches 0.448 m. north of the joint with the second block (0.448 m. at the east side and 0.446 m. at the west side), and so 1.826 m. north of the bottom of the orthostate course.

The vertically set, marble filler block, slightly trapezoidal in front elevation, which was especially made to close the awkward exterior joint between the western façade of the Propylon and the Pelasgian wall, has been ignored previously.[36] It was painstakingly carved to fit required conditions exactly; its dimensions are 0.471 m. (top), 0.567 m. (bottom), 1.768 m. (left side), and

[35] Dinsmoor had recognized that this construction was not original, but he considered the anta as having belonged to the original construction and as having been slightly relocated during the rebuilding. His idea of its original location, with its back aligning more or less with the joint cutting for the anta wall at the west end of the western orthostate, forced him to place the front face of the anta a considerable, and most uncanonical, distance behind the front edge of the stylobate.
[36] Weller, 1904, p. 42, refers to it merely as a piecing out of the poros blocks of the parastas.

1.782 m. (right side); the right edge has a northern upward slope, of 0.151 m., to fit against the outward batter of the Pelasgian wall; the left edge again has a northern upward slope, of 0.055 m., to match the similar and parallel slope of the orthostates of the flank wall inside the building (Pls. 11:D-D, 21:b, 22:b, 23:a). Not only is the slope of the left edge of this exterior block to all intents and purposes the same as that of the interior orthostates, but it lies within 0.003 m. of being on the projected plane of the face of the orthostates (i.e. it is on the line of the interior wall if that wall were extended through the parastas).[37] In addition, the outer, west face of the trape-zoidal filler block, unlike the later poros blocks of the parastas which now abut it and which slope inwards to the east, is vertical and therefore parallel to the vertical joint which was cut for the other side of the same early parastas on the western orthostate inside the building (Pl. 10). Furthermore, the level of the northern top corner of this block, which as I have already noted lies in the extended plane of the inner orthostates, is at the same elevation as the top of the string course which caps the top of the orthostates (144.576 m. *vs.* 144.581 m.; Pl. 11:C-C, D-D). In the original construc-tion, therefore, this similarity of levels would have allowed a continuous joint to be carried around the missing marble anta and anta wall to connect neatly the jointing of these still extant original parts of the building. There can be no doubt that this trapezoidal marble block belonged to the original parastas and is the sole survivor of that wall, having escaped Persian damage because of its relatively protected corner location.

In plan, the block is triangularly shaped; its right edge, however, has a return of 0.007 m. before it turns at an acute angle. This angled, hidden face against the Pelasgian wall is smoothly worked for 0.03 m., after which the surface is roughly finished (Pl. 13).

When the block was set in place, the now northernmost extant metope which lined the early forecourt was not completely removed but was cut down to the level of the stylobate, part of it underlying the parastas and part of it exposed in the area of the forecourt (Pls. 9, 12). The top surface of the metope was worked down at its northern end, under the trapezoidal filler, to the finished level of the stylobate; here, at the top of the northern end, there is a rectangular cutting, 0.095 m. high and 0.033 m. wide, the purpose of which is obscure (Pls. 12:X–X, 13). In order to match visually the thin strip of protective surface which had been retained along the west edge of the stylobate, the top of the cut-down metope along its exposed western edge was given a somewhat similar treatment; the effect is almost that of an angled, southwestern return of the stylobate (Pls. 9, 13, 23:b).

Above the trapezoidal marble filler block of the parastas there was originally a second, similar one (Pl. 15) in the area now filled with small poros blocks (Pl. 11). The face of the Pelasgian wall was worked down to present a more uniform surface for the abutting of this upper block. At the level which the top of the missing block would have reached, there is a ledge cutting, to the south, in a boulder of the Pelasgian wall (Pls. 10, 11:C-C, 15). This ledge has a maximum north-south dimension of 0.795 m. and a maximum width, to its irregular eastern edge, of 0.23 m. It has a gently downward slope to the south of 0.035 m., but this may have been caused by some slight settlement of the boulder during demolition of the Propylon. The elevation of the ledge at its northern limit is 3.49 m. above that of the finished stylobate and thereby allows for the upper, missing filler-block heights of 1.722 m. at its northern edge and 1.708 m. at its southern one (as-suming its top to be horizontal). The left, or northern vertical edges of the lower and upper filler blocks therefore varied in height by only 0.046 m. The purpose of the ledge seems evident. Below

---

[37] The orthostate is 1.076 m. at its bottom and 1.065 m. at its top from the back of the present anta. The north edge of the trape-zoidal filler block at the corresponding elevations lies 1.073 m. and 1.062 m. from the back of the present anta.

it, because of the interference of the Pelasgian wall, normal corner bonding of the front and side walls was impossible. At the level of the ledge, which was cut down 0.45 m. into the boulder of the early wall, the seventh masonry course of the gate building's façade (i.e. the one above the two corner filler blocks, 3.49 m. above the stylobate) was extended to the south to bond into the Pelasgian wall, to lend stability to the structure. The ledge cutting extends 1.515 m. south of the inner face of the side wall of the Propylon (at this level), and so *ca.* 0.715 m. beyond the southern outer limit of the building (Pl. 15). The cutting in the boulder seems to prove that the Pelasgian wall at this point, and at this time, reached no higher than the top of the boulder on which the cutting was made. Above this point, the remaining courses of the front and side walls of the Propylon were free to be bonded at the corner in normal fashion.

The working of the interior vertical joint on the western marble orthostate of the flank wall, for the reception of the inner corner of the original parastas, has already been discussed (p. 42 above). Like the exterior face of the trapezoidal filler block, it is vertical. We are therefore provided with the thickness of the original anta wall of the Propylon. The trapezoidal block of the outer face lies 0.085 m. within the western line of the stylobate. The line of the joint on the orthostate for the inner face of the wall lies 0.162 m. within the eastern line of the stylobate. Since the stylobate is 1.175 m. wide, the wall had a depth of 0.928 m., as opposed to that of the later poros wall of 0.736 m. (Pls. 4, 13). The original anta (since one presumably existed) must, by necessity, have been thicker than the wall behind it, and, therefore, the present anta, with a lower depth of only 0.835 m., must be excluded from having belonged to the original construction. This greater depth of the original anta and anta wall also explains the depth from front to back of the working down of the protective surface of the stylobate.

RECONSTRUCTION OF THE SECOND STAGE

Every previous reconstruction of the Propylon has incorporated all of the building components which are now still standing at the southwest corner of the building. No effort has been made to distinguish the periods. These restored drawings, therefore, all of which include the anta and anta wall of the post-Persian, or third stage, represent in reality the various conceptions of the appearance of the building in its last phase, rather than in its original one. This fact, however, has never been brought forth, and the unwitting reader is given the impression that the structure had only one phase and that the restored drawings represent an unchanged appearance of the Propylon from its inception until its final demolition.

Except within general guide lines, the restoration of the Propylon in its second stage (and the modifications to its design in the later, third stage, as well) cannot be exact, because of insufficient information. A basic element of the plan, which had been omitted in the restorations of Dörpfeld, Michaelis, Choisy, Weller, and the earlier plan of Stevens, but suggested in Robertson's and in Dinsmoor's texts and included in the later plan of Stevens and in that of Bundgaard, is the gate wall. Such a wall, as located by Bundgaard on the 1.70 m. wide ledge at the head of the steps, thereby creating a west and an east hall on either side of it, is a necessity. Without a gate wall, there would be no way to close the entrance to the Akropolis, and a gate building without a porch, or hall, on either side of the wall would have been most unusual.[38] The little propylon for the Sanctuary of Demeter at Selinous, which served as a parallel for some of the earlier restorations of our building, was exceptional in not having a gate, or gates. The shallow revised scheme of Stevens, on

---

[38] Similar plans were evolved from very early periods: in the second city of Troy; at Knossos; at Tiryns; and then, closer to our period, at the temple of Aphaia at Aigina. They continued right along afterwards at Sounion, the Pompeion at Athens, Eleusis, etc.

the other hand, which does have a gate wall, but shows it sandwiched between the west stylobate and the wide rock-cut ledge to the east, resulted from a misunderstanding on his part (see p. 13 above).

After the discussions between Dinsmoor and Bundgaard in September of 1939 in Copenhagen, which later led to the latter's reopening of area IV, Bundgaard in general accepted the restoration of the plan of the building as it was presented to him;[39] his restored plan[40] is therefore fairly closely in accord with our own. The controlling elements of the plan are, for the depth of the west porch, a dimension of 12.45 m. from the outer edge of the western stylobate to the center of the ledge which must have held the gate wall, and a maximum depth between the outer faces of the west and east stylobates of *ca.* 16.80 m. dictated by the fact that the southern flank wall, extended to the east, must have ended within the building limits of the later Propylaia since there exist no cuttings in the bedrock outside the later building; for the width, a minimum interior dimension, between the face of the south flank wall and the northernmost exposed limit of the bedrock cutting in area IV, of 16.80 m. The following table gives comparisons between similar parts of the Propylon and the later Propylaia:

West anta to center of gate wall (Propylaia): 12.3895 m. (N) and 12.3815 m. (S)
West anta to center of gate wall (Propylon): 12.395 m. (12.450 − 0.055)
Between outer faces of antae (Propylaia): 16.446 m.
Max. between outer faces of antae (Propylon): 16.690 m. (16.80 − 2×0.055)
Interior width between flank walls (Propylaia): 18.140 m.
Min. interior width between flank walls (Propylon): 16.800 m.

Inasmuch as the east-west dimensions of the Propylon, between the outer faces of the antae and between these outer faces and the center of the gate wall, closely approximate those of the later Propylaia, we should be fairly safe in assuming, as does Bundgaard,[41] a north-south width of building slightly greater than the minimum possible limit, which also approximates that of the Propylaia (see Pl. 15 for my various schemes employing minimum and maximum widths). Since the width of the flank walls of the Propylon, *ca.* 0.80 m., is not very different from that of the outer walls of the Propylaia, 0.88 m., we can hypothesize a similar width of gate wall for the two buildings; in fact, the great width of the rock cutting under the gate wall of the Propylon demands a heavy wall such as was used for the Propylaia. Based on these assumptions, we can postulate for the Propylon the following dimensions, which meet the controlling limitations (see Pls. 14–16):

circa

Between outer faces of west and east stylobates: 16.550 m. 50 5/8 D.F.
Between outer faces of west and east antae : 16.440 m. 50 5/16 D.F.
Depth of west hall : 11.755 m. 36 D.F.
Width of gate wall : 1.280 m. 3 15/16 D.F.
Depth of east hall : 3.405 m. 10 3/8 D.F.
Interior width between flank walls : 18.140 m. 55 1/2 D.F.
Total width of building : 19.740 m. 60 3/8 D.F.

The steps between the lower and upper levels in the eastern half of the gatehouse have posed problems for all of the various restorers (Pl. 5). The difference in level of bedrock is 1.157 m. Four risers of 0.300 m. each (as compared to 0.314 m. and 0.324 m. for the top two steps of the outer

[39] Bundgaard, 1957, p. 9, where the date is wrongly given as 1937.
[40] Bundgaard, 1957, figs. 22, 40.
[41] Bundgaard, 1957, p. 44.

krepidoma) work ideally, and allow at the back of the threshold a stop for the gates, 0.04 m. high (Pl. 14). A four-step solution was presented by Bundgaard,[42] in which he tried to utilize the bedrock surfaces as finished steps as much as possible, filling these cuttings out with blocks. He made several mistakes, however, which nullify his solution.[43]

We have already concluded that the cut-down bedrock of the floors and steps was merely a dressed subsurface, over which marble slabs and step blocks were either placed or were planned to be placed. The cuttings for the steps are much too irregular, both in height and depth, to have served in their present form as a stair. Also, the slight irregularities in the heights of these rock-cut beddings would indicate joints in superposed blocks. The controlling eastward limit for the placing of the lowest finished riser is the lowest rock-cut ledge, 0.222 m. high, at its southern exposed end. This lies 10.58 m. from the outer edge of the western stylobate. Since the indication at the west end of the building is that the floor slabs had a thickness of 0.146 m., their tops would have been 0.076 m. below the lowest rock-cut step of the gate-wall stair. This juncture of the two materials must have been covered over by a slightly westwardly overlapping finished step. We do not know precisely the point where this first riser was placed, but the clearance between its approximate location, as shown on Plate 14, and the west face of the gate wall should, and does, allow for four canonical steps with risers of 0.30 m. each (1.20 m.) and treads of 0.40 m. each (1.20 m.). The finished floor in the east hall is then stepped down *ca.* 0.04 m. below the level of the top step, or sill, to give a stop for the valves of the doors, and continues to the east stylobate with slabs on top of the leveled bedrock, 0.146–0.149 m. thick (Pl. 14). East of the gate building, beyond the further-most possible limit of the stylobate of the east façade, the bedrock again rises. It would appear, therefore, that for purposes of preventing cascading ground water from flowing into the building a raised stylobate, acting as a dam, must have been employed here, with a slightly more primitive design, probably, than the one used later for the Propylaia.

Finally, in regard to the interior steps, inasmuch as the only rock-cut traces for them that are exposed, and on the basis of which we restore the stair across the north and south aisles, lie in the area of the central aisle of the Propylon, we are forced to conclude that steps, rather than a ramp, existed here as well, and ran across the entire building.[44] Furthermore, as in the Propylaia, a ramp is definitely excluded to the east of the gate wall since the central opening of that wall required doors, and the valves of that door needed a solid floor to support them as they were opened and closed.[45] It is highly probable, however, that there was a ramp in the west hall, leading up through the central aisle.

Turning now to the west façade, we have already shown that the anta wall of this phase had a thickness of 0.928 m. It lay 0.085 m. back from the outer edge of the stylobate (based on the marble trapezoidal filler block) and certainly was composed of marble blocks with heights similar

---

[42] Bundgaard, 1976, fig. 89, although in Bundgaard, 1957, pp. 36–37, fig. 40, he strongly advocated five steps.

[43] In Bundgaard, 1957, fig. 22, using the Kavvadias-Kawerau framework of elevations, which are *ca.* 0.57 m. too high above sea level, Bundgaard's relationship of elevations to each other for the western stylobate, for the later floor slab just back of the stylobate, for the bedrock cutting under the gate wall, and for the bedrock surface east of that (143.38, 143.29, 143.85, and 144.47 m.) are approximately correct. In Bundgaard, 1976, fig. 89, he erroneously identified his elevation + 143.29 m., which belonged to the later floor slab, as belonging to the stylobate, thereby lowering that course 0.09 m. (143.38–143.29). In this way, he optimistically obtained two lower risers for the gate-wall stair of 0.29 m. each, to match his two upper risers of the same stair of 0.30 m. each (by his own earlier, and more correct figures, the two lower risers should have been only 0.245 m. each). Furthermore, in his figure 89, he shows the third riser of his stair in line with the west face of the gate wall, and the first riser *ca.* 0.80 m. west of that. This first riser, then, bites into and conflicts with the extant first bedrock step (which he does not show) for an amount of 0.43 m. (see Pl. 14).

[44] Bundgaard (1957, fig. 40) omits stairs here, but in Bundgaard, 1976, fig. 89, he does show them in the elevation of the building.

[45] The problem which Mnesikles faced with his central doors will be discussed in the second volume of this study.

to those of the later poros ones, but coursed more uniformly to level out with the top of the exterior corner trapezoidal filler block and the top of the interior string course, and also with the higher ledge cutting in the Pelasgian wall. The outer face of the presently standing anta is set back 0.055 m. from the edge of the stylobate, snugly occupying the western limit of the finished area where the protective surface of the stylobate had been removed; this must also have been the location of the outer face of the original anta, since the set-back from the protective face of the stylobate of 0.055 m. (0.050 m. to finished face) is standard in Greek Doric construction. The projection of the anta outside the face of the wall is then 0.03 m. If one repeats this projection on the interior face, the original anta would have had a depth of 0.928 + 2(0.030) = 0.988 m. Since the depth of antae and the lower diameter of adjacent columns bore a close similarity in Greek design, we may assume that the columns of the original façade had a lower diameter of 0.988 m.[46] From this point, one must continue with analogies.

Based on the proportion of the lower diameter of our columns to those of the following buildings, the spacings and heights of the columns of the following buildings, altered to be proportional to our lower diameter, would be as follows:

	Spacing	Height	Height in lower Diameters
Athenian Treasury at Delphi (507 B.C.):	2.831 m.	5.373 m.	5.44
Athena Pronaia at Delphi (*ca.* 500 B.C.):	2.443 m.	4.522 m.	4.58
Poseidon (old) at Sounion (498 B.C.) :	2.469 m.		
Aphaia at Aigina (*ca.* 495–485 B.C.) :	2.615 m.	5.267 m.	5.32
Propylaia (Wings) (437 B.C.) :	2.305 m.	5.383 m.	5.45

We can therefore assume a column height of *ca.* 5 1/3 lower diameters, or 5.270 m. (Pl. 14). This height also agrees with the height of the equivalent of three of the southwest corner trapezoidal filler blocks against the Pelasgian wall, or nine courses of blocks for the anta wall (Pl. 15). The spacing of the columns, however, is more problematical. In Plate 15 are shown six tentative schemes for the west elevation of the Propylon, using four and six columns and both the minimum and maximum widths of façade. As can be seen, in no scheme, except A, can the triglyphs be made to work both in regard to the entire width of the building and to the columns and antae, but in this scheme A the columns are much too closely spaced and they leave no room for the passage of the Panathenaic procession.[47] Scheme B, with basic column spacings of 2.725 m. and a central spacing half again as wide, is satisfactory except that the end metopes are impossibly narrow. In scheme C, with a uniform frieze, a floating triglyph which pays no regard to the anta below, as at the propylon of the Demeter sanctuary at Selinous, is shown, but the irregularity of the column spacings and column-to-anta spacings is impossible. Scheme D, utilizing the minimum width of façade, with basic column spacings of 2.481 m. and a central spacing half again as wide, has the same fault with the corner metopes as does B. Schemes E and E', with regularly spaced

---

[46] Bundgaard obviously believed that his large columns, with a lower diameter of 1.065 m., were original and continued, undamaged, down to 437 B.C. when, he would lead us to believe, they were re-used again in the Mnesiklean Propylaia (Bundgaard, 1976, pp. 154–155). He ignores the evidence of fire damage and refutes a rebuilding of the Propylon (Bundgaard, 1957, p. 33, note 25).

[47] In Weller's distyle-in-antis *narrow* plan, the triglyphs seemingly align properly with the columns, the now extant anta, and the corners of the building. Although he did not work it out for us mathematically, his center columns are 3.4905 m. on center, his metopes are 0.699 m. wide, and the two end metopes are increased by 0.016 m. in width to 0.715 m. Weller did not, however, take into consideration the diminution in width of the anta at its top nor the inward slope of the flank walls. Therefore, in actuality, his center columns should be 3.483 m. on center, his metopes should be 0.696 m. wide, and the two end metopes, in turn, must be decreased by 0.049 m. in width to 0.647 m., which is *not* such a pleasant solution.

triglyph friezes of two different sizes and a normal central columnar spacing, are out of the question since there is no proper relationship between the triglyphs and columns. Other minor permutations of these schemes are possible, but they lead to no better results. We are therefore forced to accept a slightly variant design in which the triglyph frieze did not extend to the corners of the building, but stopped above the antae (Pl. 15:B').[48] Whether this variant solution should be based on the wide scheme B or the narrow scheme D is somewhat conjectural, but based on other similarities to the later Propylaia, the wider scheme is shown here in the restored drawing (Pl. 16). Also, the ratio of the resulting height of the entire order in scheme B to the height of the columns, *ca.* 1.36:1, is completely in accord with comparable buildings.[49]

To hold up the ceiling and roof, there must have been two rows of columns in the west hall, just as in the later Propylaia. This necessity had been recognized only by Stevens (Pl. 5). Ionic columns are out of the question, since the first employment we know of such columns in a Doric building on the mainland of Greece is in the later Parthenon.[50] A superposed order is impossible, since the intervening epistyle course between the two orders would by necessity have had to frame into the shafts of the central columns of the west façade. We are left, then, with single Doric columns which must have been higher than the outer ones, partly because the epistyle course above them needed a ledge on which to rest at the west (upon the epistyle of the façade) but primarily because the same epistyle course had to be high enough at the east to allow space for properly proportioned doors in the gatewall (Pl. 14). The proportion of height to lower diameter of these columns would probably have been greater than that of the outer ones, since it would have been most unpleasant, and uncanonical, to have had thicker shafts inside than out. An analagous situation obtained in the venerable Royal Stoa in the Athenian Agora where the interior columns had a much smaller diameter than had the outer ones; in this case the inner columns had the same height as the outer ones, but their proportion of height to lower diameter was much greater than was that of the columns of the façade, 7.05:1 *vs.* 5.10:1.[51] One must also, of course, consider the possibility that neither the roof and ceiling construction nor these interior supports of the original Propylon were ever erected. Even if such were the case, however, the entire construction must already have been planned.

Since the eastern stylobate of the building was raised about 1.50 m. above that at the west, and since the columns of both façades must have maintained approximately the same height, the roof and ceiling of the east porch must have been raised about 1.50 m. above the corresponding elements of the west porch, in a manner similarly employed in the Propylaia (Pls. 14, 15:B'). The break in the roof lines would have occurred over the gatewall.

DATE OF THE SECOND STAGE

There exists little tangible evidence for the date of the original construction of the old gatehouse. In the past, it has been assigned anywhere from the Peisistratid to the Kallikratean period.

---

[48] Bundgaard obviously came to the same conclusion (Bundgaard, 1976, fig. 89), but he restored an unparalleled number of four metopes over his central columns in order to obtain a clear spacing between those columns of 4 meters, a dimension slightly greater even than that employed between the central columns of the larger Propylaia. What is more amazing is that Bundgaard trustingly spanned his 4-meter clear opening with an epistyle of only 0.80 m. in height, while Mnesikles, with a similar span for the Propylaia, was worried about the capability of his much stronger epistyle, which had a height of 1.14 m., and hollowed out the inner, central part of the members of his epistyle to lighten them.

[49] See Dinsmoor, 1950, tables after p. 340.

[50] The two orders had been combined earlier in the colonies, in the temple of Athena at Paestum, but there the Ionic columns were used outside, for the front porch.

[51] Shear, 1971, pp. 243–250.

What is known now for certain is that it fell, in time, between the building of the forecourt and the rebuilding of the gatehouse after fire damage.

The only tangible evidence lies in the workmanship of the marbles, but it does not tell us much. The type of stippled panels with flush, smooth borders which appear on the risers and treads of the steps and on the face of the orthostates was standard for a long period of time in the 5th century. It was used both as a temporary decorative treatment of protective surfaces (later to be removed) and as a permanent decoration. It appears on the column drums of the older Parthenon and, more than forty years later, appears again on the back of the stylobate blocks of the Hephaisteion and on the front of the steps and back of the stylobate blocks of the temple of Poseidon at Sounion. Only three years after the completion of the latter temple, a slightly different appearance was given to this type of panel on Mnesikles' Propylaia, where the stippling is coarser and the smooth borders are a bit recessed; but at this self-same time the earlier, more delicate type appears again on the antae of the propylaia at Sounion. It would seem to be impossible to pinpoint the date of a structure from the treatment of these panels, the types of treatment obviously having been selected at the whim of the individual architect, but Bundgaard attempts to do so and considers the more delicate type of paneling to be uniquely Kallikratean.[52] He surprisingly assigns both the old Parthenon and the old Propylon to Kallikrates, after 457 B.C. Inexplicably, he considers the paneling of the Propylon to be the final, finished treatment of the marble.[53]

As mentioned before, the protective surface at the back of the treads of the krepidoma is worked down to the finished surface of the steps. No such provision, however, was made at the bottom of the risers, although the protective surfaces of both planes were obviously intended to be removed eventually. This somewhat illogical and primitive treatment of the problem is taken here as an indication of earlier, rather than later, workmanship. Then, again, at the vertical corner between the original parastas and the orthostates within the gate house, a similar primitive treatment must have obtained, where neither plane was worked down beforehand to the finished surface; this situation would have caused difficulties for the final finishers of the building, had the work been completed.

The only possible way to arrive at a date for the initial construction of the gate building is by logical analysis of the problem. If we accept the early 480's as the time when the Hekatompedon metopes became available, and therefore as the time when the forecourt was built, the Propylon must be later than that date. To assign it to a period as late as the mid-450's, however, as does Bundgaard, is untenable; this would mean that within a span of about 18 years, prior to the beginning of the work on the Propylaia in 437 B.C., the building was erected, destroyed, re-erected, and then dismantled. A Kimonian date in the 460's, although somewhat more plausible, must also logically be discarded on the same grounds as was the Kallikratean date. It would be difficult to find a cause for fire-destruction of the Propylon in the post-Kimonian period,[54] and a construction and then a reconstruction of this impressive edifice during a period of some 28 years is hard to imagine. We must next consider the decade of the 470's, immediately after the Persian wars, when Athens was exhausted. Although work on fortifications proceeded, financed largely by monies obtained from Athens' allies, this era, very understandably, is notable for its lack of monumental buildings, and we can therefore hardly justify assigning to it a construction of such grandiose proportions and materials. We must, then, return to the 480's as the only logical time interval in

---

[52] Bundgaard, 1976, pp. 50–53.

[53] Bundgaard, 1976, p. 50.

[54] War and civil strife are ruled out, and one would certainly not expect to find tapestries and oil lamps, which in combination appear to have been the cause of most fires in temples, in a utilitarian gate building.

which a monument such as ours could conceivably have been erected, at a time, in fact, which serves very well as one for the Propylon as part of a greater building program, in conjunction with the erection of the older Parthenon. Just as the Classical Parthenon and Propylaia were erected simultaneously so that the great temple to Athena would have a fitting approach, so would the Archaic Parthenon and Propylon have been put up together. And just as the Classical Parthenon was actually begun some years before ground was broken for the Propylaia, such would have been the sequence for their predecessors. If we accept 488 B.C. as the year when the older Parthenon was started, we can consider the construction during that same year of the forecourt to the Mycenaean gate as a makeshift embellishment of the entrance to the Akropolis.[55] This latter, after all, was a fairly minor operation. Then, after a short time, the new gatehouse was planned and the steps of the krepidoma were erected as a first stage. A delay ensued, for unknown reasons, after which the hampering parts of the Pelasgian wall were removed and work on the Propylon was continued. By this point we must be fairly well down into the 480's, not too long before the Persian attack. It is most probable, therefore, that the gatehouse was not completed by 480 B.C., any more than was the older Parthenon, and that both of them were burned by the Persians while still in their unfinished state.

THE THIRD STAGE: THE REBUILDING

Traces of repairs have frequently been noted in the Propylon.[56] After its destruction by fire, it was repaired and partly rebuilt. Some of the original construction, such as the krepidoma and the lower part of the flank walls, was re-usable. Much of it, however, had to be supplemented by new and secondhand material. The appearance of the gatehouse during this phase is the more difficult one to envisage since, although the general outlines of the structure were certainly the same as before, the new building elements would seem not to have fitted canonical proportions of the period, and the only evidence we have for the construction is what now remains in area II. The antae, and probably the columns as well, were much more slender than in the original work and therefore no longer sat squarely centered on the stylobate, and a mishmash of poros and marble was used. This, then, is the Propylon which Mnesikles finally tore down in 437 B.C.

THE FLOOR AND WALL BENCHES

I have suggested earlier that the paving slabs for the floor of the original Propylon were never completely installed, although we shall never know to what extent this part of the work was completed, since the floor of the west hall would have lain more than 0.10 m. higher than that of the later Propylaia and the floor of the east hall would have been at the same level as that of the later building. Both floors would necessarily have been removed in their entirety in 437 B.C. Whether the floor was placed or not, and, if so, whether part of it was utilized again in the later rebuilding, we do know that at the southwest corner of the building a new floor was installed, stepped down 0.072 m. below the intended finished level of the stylobate, or 0.076 m. below its protective surface, at elevation +142.736 m.

[55] I still firmly believe that the Hekatompedon, which supplied the metopes for the forecourt, underlay the older Parthenon and had to be demolished to make way for that construction (Dinsmoor, 1947, pp. 109–151; cf. Travlos, 1971, p. 258).

[56] Miller, 1893, p. 519; Dörpfeld, 1897, p. 167, and 1902, pp. 405–406; Weller, 1904, p. 67; D'Ooge, 1908, p. 77; Köster, 1909, pp. 27, 29, note 2, 32; Dörpfeld, 1911b, pp. 93–94; Judeich, 1931, p. 67.

One marble slab of this flooring still exists, almost *in situ* but shifted a little to the east during the building of the Propylaia (0.009 m. at the north corner and 0.004 m. at the south). Because of this shift, the slab, which rests on rubble packing (Pls. 11:C–C, 12), subsided 0.010 m. at its western end (Pl. 9).[57] The underpacking was necessary since the block is only 0.164 m. thick and there was left an empty gap below it (above the now covered northern extension of the top rock-cut step of the early forecourt) of 0.16 m. Only for the southeast corner of this block was any cutting of bedrock required, where the leveled bedrock for the subflooring of the original Propylon interfered (Pls. 9, 19:b). The slab itself was secondhand, re-used after its probable original employment as a supporting base of some sort. Two sides of the block are treated in euthynteria fashion with a roughened, projecting surface starting 0.08 m. below the top, as if the stone had originally been set partially below ground level. The top surface, which is slightly out of square, 0.898–0.899 m. × 1.200–1.209 m., has chiseled borders 0.15 to 0.18 m. wide, while the inner field is picked. There is no possibility that this was carved originally as a flooring slab.[58]

Also at this time, the two lower courses of the flank wall were considerably altered. It is likely that they were heavily calcined by fire and had to be cut down. The upper course, which probably originally formed a bench, was hacked back to the line of the upper orthostates. The lower course, which had been the raised platform under the original bench and had a total height of 0.38 m., was cut down 0.05 m. at the top and cut back 0.285 m. at the front, but only for the upper vertical height of 0.256 m. (Pls. 4:D_1, 17). The total original depth of the lower course (front to back) was maintained at the bottom of the blocks for a height of 0.074 m., at elevation + 142.736 m., which is the same elevation as that of the adjacent floor slab. This thin protruding lip of the strangely shaped, cut-down block therefore formed part of the new flooring. Although this lip is now mostly broken away, the break line is clearly visible at the bottom of the later benches (the second and third original platform blocks from the west) and the entire thickness of this thin, later floor is preserved on the western corner block (Pls. 10, 19:b). The new, finished surfaces of these two lower courses, including that of the floor, are very roughly picked, presenting an extremely crude appearance. No other floor slabs exist, but their finish could hardly have matched that of either the single, re-used block of the floor or the roughly picked finish of these cut-down platform blocks. They would probably again have been secondhand marbles, and must have produced a pavement which looked like a patchwork quilt.

The cut-down bench of this last phase is unusually low, 0.256 m. as compared with 0.272 m. and 0.292 m. for the earlier interior bench and the exterior seat blocks of the forecourt. It may be that another course of thin slabs was superposed above to give it the additional height of a few centimeters, and this possibility is strengthened by two pieces of evidence. One of these is the occurrence of two pry cuttings on top of the second bench block, near its west end (Pl. 9); it may seem strange that pries would be required for setting such thin marbles in place, but we have exactly the same situation on top of the orthostates where there are pry cuttings which were used in conjunction with the thin slabs of the string course. The other piece of evidence is a shallow cutting, 0.345 m. wide, which occupies the full height of the cut-back second course of the flank wall (beneath the joint between the orthostates) and extends 0.046 m. down into the first course (Pls. 10, 19:a). This cutting must have helped to anchor a votive offering which rested on the

[57] Weller, 1904, pp. 41, 55, states that the slab is *in situ*.

[58] And yet Weller, 1904, pp. 37, 41–42, 55, considered the block to be one of a whole series of identical flagging stones which lay in rows of nine abreast, and many earlier investigators considered it to be an ordinary floor slab: Bohn, 1882, p. 16b; Milchhöfer, 1885, p. 201; Bötticher, 1888, p. 89; Judeich, 1905, p. 208, and 1931, p. 226; D'Ooge, 1908, pp. 74, 76; Fougères, 1911, p. 40. The roughened, euthynteria-like projection below the upper finished sides of the block immediately prevents it from ever having abutted tightly with other blocks.

westernmost bench block (before it was later cut away). One would suppose that such an object would have been set down into the top of the bench for additional stability. The wall cutting terminates at the presently existing level of the seat blocks to the east, however, and there could have been no anchorage in the top of the bench unless a separate capping course had existed.

During this phase, the inner face of the later (present) anta wall lay further west than did the original one (see below). As a result, between the western end of the first bench block and this wall there was a gap, which may have been filled in with a small, additional block.

Finally, in regard to the bench, the westernmost block was inexplicably cut away later, during some period in the last phase of the Propylon (Pl. 4:D). The level of the later floor in front of this bench was now continued all the way back to the wall, so that the entire horizontally exposed part of the block, at its western half, is only 0.074 m. thick. Beginning at about its midpoint, the block was chipped down still further, towards the east, to a thickness of only 0.042 m.; this portion is so thin that it was easily shattered and is now partially broken away (Pls. 9, 10, 18:a). In the area which had been occupied by the bench, a cutting was now made in the newly formed floor, 0.317 m. wide and 0.299 m. from front to back. Its floor thickness is only 0.023 m. Since its width is so similar to that for the dedication which had rested originally on the bench, and since it lies almost directly below the cutting in the wall, one wonders if this later depression was not made to hold the same object which once rested on the bench in an earlier period (Pl. 19:a). Since it is centered about 0.05 m. further west than the upper one, the two cuttings could not have been used simultaneously.[59] A minor problem also arose during this remodeling work: with the removal of the western bench, the entire trapezoidal gap at the south end of the stylobate was exposed, disclosing the slot which had contained the metope of the early forecourt, and also disclosing the bedrock behind it (Pls. 4:D, 18:a). This hole was therefore covered with a marble slab, 0.057 m. thick, a remnant of which still remains at the foot of the flank wall (Pl. 18:b).

In 437 B.C. the east part of the third bench block was cut back diagonally by Mnesikles, on the same line as the krepidoma, to make way for the Propylaia (Pl. 20:b).

THE ANTA AND ANTA WALL

On the stylobate now stand two blocks of a marble anta,[60] of which the north face (toward the missing columns) is 0.835 m. in width at the bottom, tapering to 0.812 m. at the present top; the side returns, parallel to the anta wall, are 0.586 m. at the bottom, tapering to 0.570 m. at the top (Pl. 11).[61] The amounts of diminution in each case are similarly related to the dimensions at the bottom of the anta, i.e. 0.023:0.835 = 0.016:0.586 = 1:*ca.* 36.5. There is no entasis: the sides are absolutely straight. The proportion 0.586:0.835 m. (or 7:10) gives exceptionally wide returns to those sides which are parallel to the walls; the proportion of side return to face of the antae of the

---

[59] Weller perceived the connection between the two cuttings, because of their identity of size and location, but he reversed their chronological order, making the cutting on the floor original, and that above the seat a later modification, supposing that a new seat block had been inserted (Weller, 1904, p. 40).

[60] A few earlier investigators, as Chaudet (1852, p. 298), Beulé (1862, pp. 43–44), Michaelis (1876, pp. 276, 278), Burnouf (1877, pp. 186–188, pls. XII:12, and XVII), and Robert (1880, p. 175), assumed that this was one jamb of a doorway. Its form, with projections both on the inside and outside, could never have been used in combination with actual doors, though a simple open gateway would be possible. Since other propyla always have open columnar façades, we may be justified in following the general theory that this is an anta.

[61] Weller gives similar measurements for the bottom (Weller, 1904, pl. II), and observes that the anta tapers (*ibid.,* p. 36); Bohn, giving 0.830 m. for the face and 0.573 to 0.580 m. for the returns (Bohn, 1882, p. 16b), evidently measured at some distance above the bottom, without observing the taper. Bundgaard (1976, p. 154) gives a constant width of 0.835 m. from bottom to top, with no taper. Plommer (1960, p. 146) gives the width as 1.175 m., misreading Weller's plate 2 from which he took the dimension.

West Wings of the Mnesiklean structure, on about the same scale, is 0.512:1.016 (or 5:10). The height of the lower block is 1.817 m. at the southwest corner, 1.812 m. at the southeast, 1.802 m. at the northwest, and 1.798 m. at the northeast; the second block is uniformly 1.721 m. high. The present height of the anta, composed of these two blocks, varies therefore from 3.538 m. to 3.519 m.[62] The reason for this difference was the inclination of the anta, both backward toward the interior of the building and laterally toward the columns. The backward inclination appears only on the outer face, while the inner, or east, face is absolutely vertical;[63] i.e., the axis was inclined by half of the diminution of 0.023 m., or 0.0115 m., in the present height of the anta. The lateral inclination was such that the face toward the columns leaned forward approximately three times the amount of the backward diminution, 0.067 m. in the present height, or a rate of 0.019 m. per meter;[64] the lateral inclination of the south edge is 0.083 m., a rate of 0.0235 m. per meter of height, and that of the axis is therefore 0.075 m. Since the bottom of the lower block was cut at an angle to the axis to form the entire inclination,[65] the top of the lower block forms a plane which is perpendicular to the axis of inclination (as was usual also for the lowest drums of inclined columns). The upper block has both beds perpendicular to the axis. There was at least a third block, now missing, since the anta required a capital. Such a capital could not be placed directly on the sloping top of the extant block, with or without a narrow necking,[66] for its moldings must have been horizontal and the visual effect created by the proximity of these moldings to the sloping joint just below would have been objectionable. Nor can we interpose a third complete, normal, block, about 1.77 m. high like the others, below the capital, without an exaggerated attenuation. The only possible solution seems to be that the capital was carved integrally on a third block of a height matching the others, on which the lowest moldings would be so far above the sloping joint that the divergence of line would not be noticeable. The total height of the anta would then have been about 3.53 + 1.77 = 5.30 m., or, more probably, about 5.27 m. to course out with that of the original Propylon, since much of the damaged earlier construction was probably still standing and was re-employed.[67] As compared with the width of the anta face, 0.835 m., this height would be almost 6 1/3 times the width. This proportion results in rather slender antae and columns for the period, but the remodeling of the structure was probably dictated to a large extent by both the horizontal and vertical dimensions of the pre-existing building and by the size of the secondhand architectural elements which were available.

[62] Bohn says that each block is 1.815 m. high (Bohn, 1882, p. 16b); Weller gives the total height as 3.515 m. (Weller, 1904, pp. 42, 56); Bundgaard gives the lower block a height of 1.82 m. (Bundgaard, 1976, p. 153).

[63] Based on wishful thinking and on the measurements of Erik Hansen, which he misinterpreted (Hansen's backward lean of 1.2 cm. applies only to the outer face), Bundgaard (1976, pp. 153–155) writes that the anta, which he states has a constant width from bottom to top, leans backwards into the building and that the center axis of the anta, if that anta were 5.86 m. high, would fall on the center of the stylobate below. Even his mathematics is optimistic, for if the anta did have a tilt, his 0.012 m. in 1.82 m. (sic) would result in an axial incline at the top of only 0.0385 m., and the center of his anta at the top would still be 0.0765 m. west of the center of the stylobate, rather than coinciding with it.

[64] Weller (1904, p. 57) noted an inclination of 0.06 m. toward the column. In measuring these inclinations we must allow for the displacement of the upper block, now shifted 0.033–0.040 m. to the north and 0.000–0.004 m. to the west.

[65] By a mathematical calculation we should obtain 0.011 m. instead of the 0.015 m. actually measured for the difference between the heights at north and south.

[66] It is thus restored by Weller, with a necking (Weller, 1904, pp. 55–56, fig. 4).

[67] Ross calculated, by means of fragments which he wrongly attributed to the entablature, that the height of the columns and antae was about 4.20–4.60 m. (Ross, 1855, p. 82). Weller estimated 5 x 0.835 = ca. 4.165 m. for the height of the anta (Weller, 1904, p. 56); besides the difficulty with his anta capital, the scale of the resulting frontal elevation seems too small (a human figure of 1.78 m. rises to the first joint of the anta; Weller's scale figure is only 1.64 m. tall). Stevens (1946, p. 80) estimates the height of anta at 4.714 m. Bundgaard (1976, p. 154) copies the columns of the West Wings of the Propylaia and gives a height of 5.86 m. The arrangement of the extant poros courses of the parastas, three to each marble block of the anta, implies that the missing marble block should be one third of, two thirds of, or equal to, each of the two extant blocks of the anta.

The extant blocks of the anta were lifted into place by iron tongs for which two holes, 0.17×0.08 m. in plan and 0.115 m. deep at the maximum, were cut on the top of each stone. They were not fastened to each other by dowels, and as a result the second block has been shifted out of place.[68] The back, toward the south, is treated as a joining surface, smooth for 0.11 m. at each edge (partly for the exposed projection beyond the wall and partly for the anathyrosis), slightly recessed and roughened for 0.02 m. more, and then all of the central part hollowed out 0.10 m. to decrease the weight (Pl. 9). Each exposed face of each block of the anta has a central picked panel which lies in the same plane with smooth, enframing borders (Pl. 11). The side and lowest borders are 0.032 m. wide, while those which carry across the horizontal intermediate joints have a width of 0.016 m. on each block. The presence of this half border at the top of the upper stone corroborates our assumption that the missing third block did not begin with a projecting fascia of a capital, but that it continued upward in the same plane with another half border and stippled panel. These picked surfaces are most probably protective surfaces, like those of the krepidoma and orthostates. As in the case of the krepidoma, therefore, we may assume that the three faces of the anta should eventually have been smoothed,[69] presumably cutting back 0.005 m. on each and reducing the total dimensions to about 0.825×0.581 m. The height of 5.27 m., apparently having been intended as 16 1/8 D.F., may now be estimated as 6.388 times the width of the anta face at the bottom, 9.07 times the finished width of the return.

Although the workmanship of the anta surfaces is very similar to that of the krepidoma and of the burnt inner orthostates, there is no possibility that the anta belonged to the original construction, since it is less deep than was the original anta wall back of it. The excellent quality of workmanship, however, compared to the crude treatment given to the interior of the building in this period, casts strong doubt on the anta having been carved for this remodeling work.[70] It is much more likely that the anta originated in another building and was adapted to this one.

It has been stated that the anta bore traces of red stucco, but after so many years of exposure I am now unable to discern such traces, and it is difficult to believe that they ever existed.[71]

The position of the new anta on the stylobate is very unusual. It is approximately centered on the joint of the stylobate, as was the earlier anta, extending 0.276 m. north and 0.310 m. south of it, and it lies a canonical 0.055 m. back from the outer face of the stylobate. Its inner return, however, lies 0.285 m. from the back line of the stylobate, a condition into which the remodelers of the Propylon were forced with their secondhand, smaller-scale material.

The present poros courses of the parastas are also the result of later rebuilding after a fire. The material of the original front wall was unquestionably marble.[72] Although it has been sometimes asserted that the poros parastas is part of the original construction of the Propylon,[73] the remarkably fresh tooling of the surfaces and the absence of traces of burning, as well as the fact that the

[68] Cf. Weller, 1904, p. 42.

[69] See footnote 71 below for the supposition that this roughening was a preparation for a coat of stucco.

[70] Dörpfeld states that the anta is of new blocks, inserted after 479 B.C. (Dörpfeld, 1902, p. 406); no evidence is given. Köster repeats this statement, as for the krepidoma (Köster, 1909, p. 29, note 2), saying that the anta shows no traces of fire.

[71] The supposition that the surfaces were stippled to receive a coat of stucco originated with Ross (1855, p. 82), repeated by Weller (1904, p. 42). Ross implied that he did not see any traces of stucco, and Weller alone (1904, pp. 42, 58) claims to have seen such traces. Curtius, mentioning red stucco on the "Pfeiler" (Curtius, 1891, p. 68), surely refers to the poros portion of the parastas. Dörpfeld said that the anta was not stuccoed (Dörpfeld, 1902, p. 406), and Dinsmoor, likewise finding no traces, was of the same opinion; the only stucco on the anta was that which accidentally overlapped at the point of contact with the poros anta wall (cf. Dörpfeld, 1911b, p. 94).

[72] Perhaps Dörpfeld's frequently repeated statement that the Propylon was "ganz aus Marmor" (Dörpfeld, 1902, pp. 405–406; cf. Luckenbach, 1905, p. 7) implies that he, too, would restore marble in the original parastas.

[73] Bohn, 1882, pp. 3, 16, who assigns it to Peisistratos; D'Ooge, 1908, p. 74, seems to call it original, with the original stucco; Bundgaard considers the entire construction to be contemporary (Bundgaard, 1957, p. 32, note 24, p. 33, note 25).

wall is much thinner than the original one and that it tilts inwards instead of being vertical, as the original one was, make it certain that this work dates from the period of the repairs.[74]

At present five courses of the poros wall are in place, and we have evidence that there were once at least seven courses. To fit the proposed restoration of the anta, there must actually have been nine courses, probably identical to the original scheme, three to each marble block of the anta.

The wall was designed to be uniform in thickness from bottom to top, and measures from 0.734 to 0.736 m. At the bottom it is set 0.037 m. inside the west face of the anta, and 0.063 m. inside the east face. As the west face of the anta tapers upward, the west face of the inclined wall follows the same slope; as a result, the inclined inner face of the wall gradually approaches the vertical inner face of the anta. At the top of the fifth course, where the anta is 0.816 m. deep, the wall continues to be 0.037 m. behind the west face of the anta, but it is only 0.044 m. from the east face. The wall would have been almost equidistant between the outer and inner faces of the anta at a height of about 0.59 m., or one wall course, above the present top of the anta, when the depth of the latter would have been 0.808 m. Evidently the wall was located with reference to the capital rather than to the bottom of the anta. That the poros wall exactly aligned with the center of the capital cannot be assumed, however, in view of the general carelessness of these repairs; we may reasonably suppose that at one poros course above the present top of the anta the wall was perfectly centered, and that the top of the next course, approximately at the bottom of the capital, was off center by 0.0025 m.

Each course of the poros anta wall, except the lowest, is treated at the bottom, on both inside and outside, with a decorative sunken margin which varies from 0.040 to 0.043 m. in height and which is 0.003 m. deep. The raised panels above these margins form a decorative rustication, which is very different from a protective surface; the reason for the omission of the margin on the lowest course is that it would have been out of place at the very bottom of the wall, since its function was solely to accentuate the joints between the courses of the wall (Pl. 21:b).[75] As will be shown below (see p. 63), these rusticated blocks were originally intended for use elsewhere on the Akropolis.

Each poros course is composed of a single block. The lowest one rests on the stylobate, although at its south end, on the inner side, it is not firmly seated but has a slight gap at its bottom; its height is 0.594 m. at the north end, against the anta, increasing to 0.598 m. at the south end on the inner side and to 0.601 m. on the outer side. The four upper courses now in place are formed by blocks the heights of which average individually 0.5735, 0.574, 0.600, and 0.603 m. (from bottom to top), but there are variations of as much as 0.003 m. in the height of any one block.

The lengths of these blocks, on the inner side of the wall, increase from 1.112 m. at the lowest course to 1.124 m. at the top of the fifth course because the space which they filled, between the inclined planes of the anta and of the back of the recessed joint cutting at the west end of the corner orthostate, varies with the differing slopes of these enframing surfaces (Pls. 11:C–C, 21:a). On the outer face of the same wall, rather than increasing in size as they ascend, the blocks decrease in length from 1.077 m. at the base of the lowest course to 1.050 m. at the top of the fifth course (Pl. 11:D–D). This reversal of order of lengths of blocks on the west side of the wall was caused again by the differing slopes of the enframing members. This time, however, although one

[74] This also was the opinion of Dörpfeld, 1911b, p. 94 ("der aus Poros neu errichteten Südwestwand").

[75] Weller recognized the ornamental character of this projecting rustication, but spoke of it as a "Werkzoll", which "is lacking only on the lowest, where its absence would not be noticed" (Weller, 1904, p. 43); as a matter of fact, the uniform surface of the lowest block projects as much as the "Werkzoll" of the upper courses.

of the enframings is still the back of the anta, the other is the north edge of the original marble trapezoidal filler block which parallels very closely the sloping face of the interior orthostates, rather than the line of the recessed joint cutting at the west end of the corner orthostate (Pl. 13). The lengths of the blocks on this outer face are therefore, in all cases, less than the ones on the inner side, but the differences in lengths vary considerably since the slope of the trapezoidal block (and of the orthostates) is greater than that of the back of the recessed joint cutting. As a result, each block, with different lengths at each one of its four horizontal edges, had to be specially cut and fitted. This was a more difficult job than the one required for the original marble blocks of the earlier parastas, for which the inner and outer lengths of each member were practically the same. The disposition and sizes of the poros blocks certainly approximate closely those of the original construction, although in this remodeled phase the horizontal jointing of the anta and of the anta wall do not align, and neither one aligns with the north, upper corner of the original trapezoidal filler block and the top of the inner string course above the orthostates, a condition which could not have occurred in the construction of the original Propylon.

A second trapezoidal marble block, which originally must have rested on the lower one that is *in situ* at the southwest, outer corner of the building, was probably damaged during the Persian fire. This was replaced during the reconstruction with small trapezoidal blocks of poros, each about one course of the parastas in height (Pls. 11:D–D, 21:b). These poros fillers continue the northward inclination of the north edge of the marble trapezoidal block, while the edges against the Pelasgian wall lean southward in the opposite direction to scribe against that early wall. The length of the lower of the two extant blocks increases from 0.471 m. at the bottom to 0.50 m. at the top, and that of the upper one increases from 0.50 to 0.563 m. The upper poros block, trapezoidal in plan as well as in elevation, has a depth of 0.47 m. and is fastened to the main poros block of the parastas by a double-T clamp 0.37 m. long. The sixth poros course of the anta wall, now missing, was certainly pieced out in a similar manner; we know from the interval between the anta and the smoothed face of the Pelasgian wall that the total length of this course increased from 1.687 m. at the bottom to 1.765 m. at the top.

The seventh course, also now missing, was different. Here we find a ledge cutting in the topmost remaining boulder of the Pelasgian wall, originally cut for the pre-Persian Propylon but obviously re-used in the rebuilding. The west face of the cutting lies 0.055 m. within the plane of the anta wall, and its bottom is 0.544 m. above the top of the fifth course; it is traceable horizontally for a length of 0.795 m., to a point 2.557 m. from the marble anta, where the boulder is broken off. The seventh poros course, therefore, was about 2.557 m. long, and was bonded into the Pelasgian wall for a length of about 0.795 m., to a point 1.515 m. back of the inner face of the side wall of the Propylon (at this level) or *ca.* 0.715 m. beyond the southern outer limit of the building.[76] As we indicated earlier for the original building of the Propylon, the boulder seems to prove that already by the 480's the Pelasgian wall at this point reached no higher an elevation than that which was reached by the top of the seventh course of the parastas.[77]

The entire construction of the marble anta and the poros anta wall, with the trapezoidal poros pieces inserted on top of the original marble one at the south end, is obviously a makeshift,

[76] Weller, who first mentioned this cutting (Weller, 1904, p. 56), interpreted it as the support for the external southwest corner of the Propylon, "which extended about 0.25 m. past the point of contact of the parastas and the Pelasgian wall." The basis of this theory evidently is the assumption that the south side wall was 0.80 m. thick (*ibid.,* pl. II). He therefore utilized only a very short amount of the length of the cutting.

[77] Weller seems to have come to a similar conclusion, though he stops the Pelasgian wall at the top of the sixth course (Weller, 1904, p. 57, fig. 4), in spite of the greater height given by the cut boulder itself. Kawerau used this cutting (Kavvadias and Kawerau, 1906, cols. 139/140, pl. H′) as evidence that the Pelasgian wall here reached no higher at the time of the Propylon than it does now.

patched together from various materials which happened to be at hand. For this reason we cannot assign great importance to the decorative character of the sunken margins on the normal blocks of the anta wall;[78] the margins are not continued on the abutting inserted filler pieces, and would therefore have impressed the eye merely as irregularities. The inserted pieces themselves, irregular in outline and of a different material from the marble trapezoidal filler block below them, would hardly have been allowed to remain visible. We have evidence that the whole was concealed under a coat of fine red stucco. No traces of the stucco now remain on the poros blocks themselves, but they were seen by several earlier observers,[79] and where the poros courses met the marble anta, which was evidently not stuccoed, there also remained red traces on the inner offset showing where the color ran over onto the marble.[80] The sunken margins of the poros courses were apparently filled up with a coarser stucco,[81] and both faces of the anta wall, from the anta to the Pelasgian wall (or, on the inner side, to the corner which was made with the inner face of the side wall), became smooth surfaces painted a brilliant red. In this manner were concealed the defects of the reconstruction after the Persian destruction.

The inner face of the poros parastas contains several sporadically placed holes, as if nails were once inserted here (Pls. 11:C–C, 21:a). Middleton seems to have taken these holes as evidence for a marble revetment of the inner face of the parastas.[82] Weller connects them with the suggestion by Ross (with regard to the holes in the south wall) that they are remains of the supports of the fetters of the Boiotians and Chalkidians mentioned by Herodotos;[83] but the Propylon, as we have noted, would hardly be an appropriate location for these.[84] As for the similar holes on the flank wall, these holes were probably used to support temporary decorations.

The thinning of the rebuilt parastas exposed the original rough joint surface at the west end of the orthostates of the flank wall for a width of 0.171–0.181 m. and, because of the fact that the rough, inner surface of the joint recedes at a different slope than does that of the face of the orthostates, the depth of the slot varies from 0.037 to 0.057 m. (Pl. 13).[85] This recess was packed with stucco mixed with small coarse pebbles (0.002–0.006 m. in diameter) in two coats (the outer one 0.013 m. thick), filling the hollow out to, and flush with, the surface of the protective face of the orthostates of the flank walls. Several patches of this stucco, adhering to the roughly tooled joint surface, still exist,[86] the lower one extending up 0.64 m. from the level of the stylobate (Pl. 10). A thinner coat of the same stucco, painted red, was continued over the badly calcined and flaked face of the orthostates of the flank walls. This final coat has now entirely disappeared, but it was noted by several earlier observers.[87]

We have already discussed the two rectangular depressions which existed for votive offerings along the south flank wall of the Propylon (pp. 55–56 above). There is a third one, as well, cut into the stylobate, adjacent to the inner face of the later poros parastas, 0.082 m. distant from the marble anta (Pl. 9). It is approximately rectangular, 0.326×0.214 m. in plan, and 0.027–0.037 m. deep. In the socket was inserted a base 0.288×0.170 m., fastened with molten lead; the base has

[78] Bohn considered that they prove that the parastas was not originally stuccoed (Bohn, 1882, p. 16).
[79] Schöll, 1841, p. 116, note; Ross, 1855, pp. 79, 82; Robert, 1880, p. 175; Bohn, 1882, p. 16b; Milchhöfer, 1885, p. 201; Bötticher, 1888, p. 89; Curtius, 1891, p. 68; Middleton, 1892, p. 29; Dörpfeld, 1902, p. 405, and 1911b, pp. 93–94; cf. Weller, 1904, pp. 42, 58, and D'Ooge, 1908, p. 74.
[80] Dörpfeld, 1911b, p. 94.
[81] Bohn, 1882, p. 16b.
[82] Middleton, 1892, pp. 15, 30.
[83] Weller, 1904, pp. 41, 65.
[84] See footnote 25, p. 43 above.
[85] The part of the slot directly next to the poros anta wall may have been partially reworked at this period (see p. 42 above).
[86] Weller, 1904, pp. 40, 67.
[87] Ross, 1855, p. 79; Bohn, 1882, p. 16b; Bötticher, 1888, p. 89; Dörpfeld, 1911b, p. 94.

now disappeared, but the lead still remains, 0.008–0.032 m. thick on the sides (the base was not perfectly centered in the socket, and was, moreover, set slightly askew). Weller wrote: "What stood here one can merely conjecture. It can hardly have been a free statue, the socket being too near the wall. It may, then, have been an inscription or a herm. The hypothesis that it was a Hermes Propylaeus is tempting."[88] The dimensions of this socket agree closely with those of the other socket in the pavement below the south flank wall and both of these cuttings seem to have been in use at the same time. We must assume, therefore, that after the restoration of the Propylon, two small stelai or pedestals of about equal size stood in this corner.[89]

RECONSTRUCTION OF THE THIRD STAGE

The form of the rebuilt structure must have resembled very closely that of the original one, with a few variations such as the lowering of the floor level by 0.072 m., the lowering of the seat along the flank walls by one course, and the reduction in depth of the antae and of the walls back of them. It seems most probable that new, or secondhand makeshift columns were employed, with a smaller diameter than the original ones to correspond with the depth of the new anta, although it is also possible that enough of the original column drums were salvageable so that they could be pieced out to restore columns of the original size; in the latter case, an epistyle of the original depth could easily have been re-employed, overhanging the new, thinner anta and anta wall on their inner side. If new, thinner columns were used, the original heights were probably retained, so that the columns would have had proportions which were more Hellenistic than early Classical in feeling (Plan A).

In order to avoid this anomaly of slender columns, Bundgaard, based on his erroneous restoration of the anta (see footnote 63, p. 57 above), suggested columns with the very large diameter (larger even than the original ones, about which he did not know) of 1.065 m., and then proposed that these columns were re-used by Mnesikles in the Wings of the Propylaia and are those which are still standing there.[90] Plommer, who misread Weller's drawing[91] and therefore gives the depth of the anta as 1.175 m. (0.835 m. in actuality), should logically have proceeded to restore columns with a comparable lower diameter, and indeed he does say that they "cannot have had a lower diameter greater than 1.2 metres."[92] This statement is more correct than he realized, since a dimension of 1.2 m. exceeds that of the total depth of the stylobate. He then continues: "If Bundgaard accepted Weller's order, as I think he ought, he would get a column rather more slender than the anta-face – 1 metre, say, in lower diameter – a column and anta only 4 metres high . . . ." This, of course, would produce a column of 4 lower diameters in height, which is an impossible proportion for this period. Plommer ends by accepting Weller's now discarded restoration of the *narrow* type of plan, distyle-in-antis, with small columns of *ca.* 4.165 m. in height and 0.835 m. in lower diameter.[93]

---

[88] Weller, 1904, p. 41; the socket was first discovered in Weller's excavation of 1901 (*ibid.,* p. 37); Weller suggests that it was connected with the holes on the inner face of the poros parastas.

[89] The stylobate directly in front of the stylobate cutting is worn by foot traffic, a phenomenon which appears at first glance to be most inexplicable in that the narrow ledge of stylobate which results here during this period, and which was now 0.072 m. above the floor, was only 0.132 m. deep, allowing little room for a foot. It would have been difficult to approach the object that closely, even with one's toes, to create such abrasion. Actually the wear must have occurred during the earlier phase of the building, before the cutting was made, when the platform under the bench continued along the flank wall, over the stylobate, to the original parastas; the worn area in question would then have been directly in front of the platform.

[90] Bundgaard, 1976, pp. 154–155.

[91] Weller, 1904, pl. 2.

[92] Plommer, 1960, p. 150.

[93] Plommer, 1960, pp. 146–147. Neither Weller nor Plommer suggested, however, that they were considering the Propylon in its reconstructed phase. The implication is that their reconstruction is of the original period.

Our evidence reveals nothing as to the form of the entablature and roof during this period, but here again the earlier construction was probably imitated. We can feel quite secure that the pediments were placed in normal fashion above the colonnaded façades and not above the ends of the building as Bundgaard would have us believe.[94] The chief difference in appearance between the original marble and the later, reconstructed structure, according to the observations of the earlier investigators, was in the color scheme. The walls of the rebuilt Propylon were apparently coated with red stucco against which marble columns, antae, and presumably entablature, stood out in contrasting white.

DATE OF THE THIRD STAGE

The exact date of this reconstruction of the Propylon has never been ascertained and probably never will be. It is improbable that Perikles would have executed such a work, because the idea of a new and imposing rebuilding of the Akropolis seems to have been always uppermost in his mind, and a rebuilding of the gate building such a short time-interval before the construction of the Propylaia makes little sense. Such a date would also have left the Akropolis without a workable entrance for more than twenty-five years after the Persian destruction. By elimination, therefore, we are forced to ascribe it either to Themistokles or to Kimon.[95]

There is only one piece of internal evidence which might shed any light upon the question of the date, and it is not very helpful. This evidence consists of the material of the poros anta wall, composed, as we have seen, of blocks with decorative sunken margins which were not originally intended to be hidden, and yet apparently were covered with stucco after they were erected in this building. We must therefore assume that the blocks were either taken from some previously existing structure, or that they were superfluous blocks, prepared for some structure which was in course of erection after 479 B.C., and used here for the sake of economy. Decorative rustication of this sort is a marked characteristic which is found in another work of about this period, the parapet of the north wall of the Akropolis, where such blocks were used from a point north of the Propylaia to a point northeast of the Erechtheion. Within this distance the parapet is preserved at four places.

The coursings of the Akropolis wall blocks vary, as do ours. In height they are 0.369, 0.414, 0.528, 0.539, 0.549, 0.553, 0.555, 0.560, 0.573, and 0.695 m. Where measurable, certain of these are 0.545 and 0.680 m. in thickness. They all have sunken margins at the bottom, usually on both sides but sometimes on one side only. These vary from 0.040 to 0.042 m. in height and are recessed 0.003 m., in exactly the same way as ours. This defensive wall constituted a large undertaking and used a great deal of material. It seems logical that our blocks were left over from this work and that the two constructions were fairly contemporary. Unfortunately, the dates to be assigned to the various parts of the Akropolis walls have never been satisfactorily determined, although it is generally agreed that all were constructed between 480 and 440 B.C.

Any theory can be argued for or against, based on the circumstantial evidence that one wants to adduce. Literary evidence informs us that Kimon built the south wall, after the battle of Eurymedon (ca. 468 B.C.),[96] and that the rest of the wall, aside from the part built by Kimon, was the

---

[94] Bundgaard, 1976, p. 155, fig. 89.

[95] Among modern authorities who mention the repairs, Dörpfeld makes no reference to the date, and Weller does not decide between Themistokles and Kimon; Miller prefers Kimon, and Köster definitely ascribes them to Kimon because of his erroneous theory that most of the marble in the Propylon is new and would hardly have been quarried immediately after the Persian invasion.

[96] Plutarch, *Cimon* 13.7; *Cimon and Lucullus* 1.5; Cornelius Nepos, *Cimon* 2.5. It is now fairly well agreed, however, that the upper part of this wall was Periklean (Dörpfeld, 1902, pp. 392, 400ff., and most recently Bundgaard, 1976, p. 76).

work of the Pelasgians.[97] The north wall follows a jagged route, constructed in nineteen planes, and this is taken as evidence that it is more primitive and therefore earlier than the south and east walls, which have long, straight stretches; but the north slope of the Akropolis is a great deal steeper and more difficult to build on than the others, so the wall followed the natural contours in much the same manner as did the Pelasgian one. Its date, however, cannot be prior to 479 B.C., since it incorporates part of the entablature of the old Athena temple and drums from the older Parthenon.

Most scholars accept the fact that these two temples were destroyed by the Persians in 480 B.C., and the idea arose that Themistokles built the wall in the 470's, along with the city walls.[98] Dörpfeld, however, temporarily decided that the older Parthenon was Kimonian,[99] and this idea led to datings of the north wall in the Periklean period,[100] or even later.[101] Then Dörpfeld returned to the view that the older Parthenon was pre-Persian and that the entire north wall was Themistoklean.[102] The seesaw has continued to move up and down ever since. Kolbe pushed for a post-Persian date of the older Parthenon in 1936.[103] Walter reverted to the pre-Persian date in 1952.[104] Carpenter, in 1970, straddled the question, accepting the pre-Persian Parthenon, but interjecting an extra, intermediate Kimonian Parthenon, built by Kallikrates during the years *ca.* 468–465 B.C., prior to the Periklean one.[105] Bundgaard, in 1976, also accepted Kallikrates as the architect of an earlier Parthenon, but he claims that this Kallikratean building was the first and only older Parthenon, with no predecessors, and that it dates in the Periklean period, after 454 B.C.[106] Bundgaard then turned to the north wall of the Akropolis which he asserts was built after 438 B.C., and later pinpoints to a date of 434/3 B.C.[107] The poros blocks with the sunken margins he considers to be re-used material, from an earlier (unspecified) date.[108]

After all these educated guesses as to the date of the north wall, although we can be fairly sure that our poros blocks of the Propylon originated with the same lot that was used in that wall, we still cannot tie them down to either the Themistoklean or the Kimonian decades. Even if the blocks were cut in the Themistoklean period, there is no evidence that the ones which were incorporated into the Propylon were utilized immediately after their arrival on the Akropolis. Dinsmoor leaned toward a Themistoklean date in the 470's B.C. for both the north wall of the Akropolis and the remodeling of the gate building. I, however, can merely reassert that there was a dearth of monumental building in the 470's in Athens, and therefore I feel that a Kimonian date in the 460's seems the most probable for the post-Persian remodeling of the Propylon.[109]

Although this date for the reconstruction is somewhat clouded because of lack of evidence, that of the demolition of the Propylon to make way for its still more glorious successor is well attested. In 437 B.C., at the height of the Periklean building program, the architect Mnesikles caused the building, which had served as the entrance to the Akropolis for some 45 years, to be pulled down. He then erected the most carefully constructed multipurpose edifice of antiquity, the Propylaia, which will form the subject matter of Part II of this study.

---

[97] Pausanias, I.28.3.

[98] Ross, 1855, pp. 126–129; Beulé, 1862, pp. 46–50; Dyer, 1873, p. 121.

[99] Dörpfeld, 1885, pp. 275–277; Dörpfeld, 1891, pl. I; Dörpfeld, 1886a, pp. 165–166, and 1886b, p. 341; Dörpfeld, 1887, pp. 32, 45; Dörpfeld, 1892, pp. 188–189.

[100] Curtius, 1891, pp. 143–144; Dörpfeld, 1892, p. 189; Michaelis, 1901, pl. XV:iv.

[101] Bötticher, 1888, p. 92 (contemporary with Erechtheion).

[102] Dörpfeld, 1902, pp. 402, 403, 412, 413; D'Ooge, 1908, pp. 44–45, 66, 70; Köster, 1909, pp. 29–31; Dickens, 1912, p. 5; Collignon, 1914, pp. 35, 38.

[103] Kolbe, 1936, pp. 1–64.

[104] Walter, 1952, pp. 97–107.

[105] Carpenter, 1970, p. 67.

[106] Bundgaard, 1976, p. 139.

[107] Bundgaard, 1976, pp. 125, 129.

[108] Bundgaard, 1976, note 293.

[109] See Boersma, 1970, p. 46 for a date of about 465 B.C. for the north wall.

GENERAL INDEX

PLATES

PLATE 1

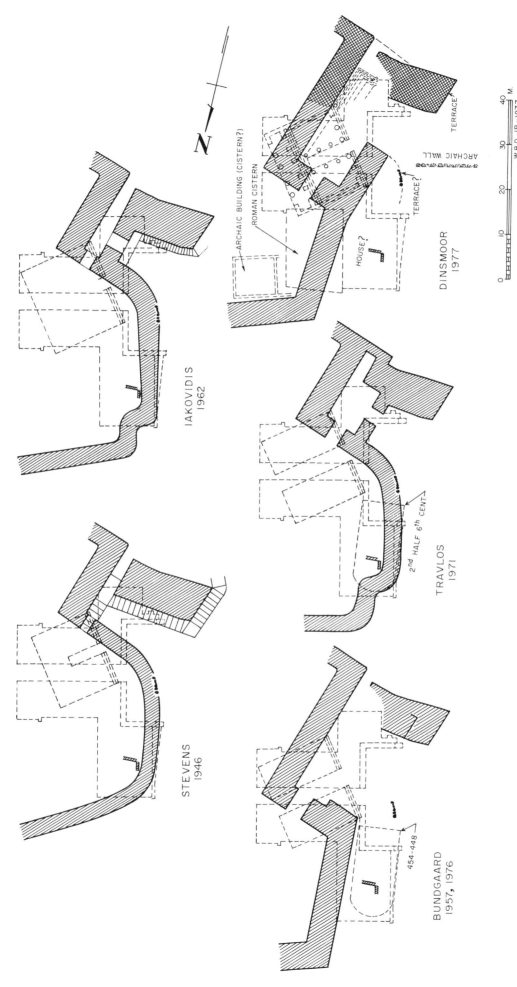

STEVENS
1946

IAKOVIDIS
1962

ARCHAIC BUILDING (CISTERN?)

ROMAN CISTERN

HOUSE?

TERRACE?

ARCHAIC WALL

TERRACE?

TERRACE?

DINSMOOR
1977

N

TRAVLOS
1971

2nd HALF 6th CENT.

BUNDGAARD
1957, 1976

454-448

W.B.D., JR.-1977

0   10   20   30   40 M.

Restorations of the Mycenaean entrance in the Pelasgian wall

PLATE 2

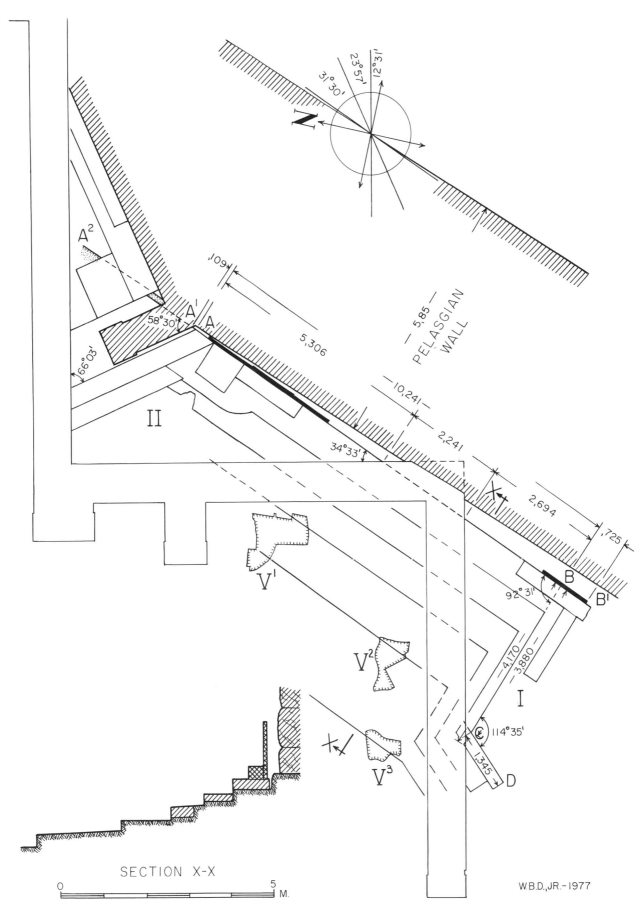

SECTION X-X

0 _____ 5 M.

Study of orientations: Propylaia, Propylon, and forecourt

W.B.D.,JR.-1977

PLATE 3

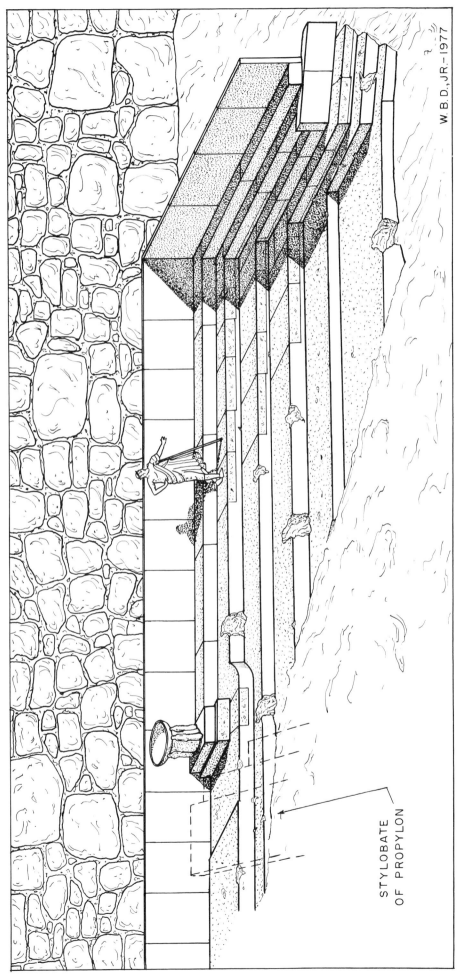

STYLOBATE
OF PROPYLON

W.B.D.,JR.-1977

Isometric view of the forecourt in its original phase

PLATE 4

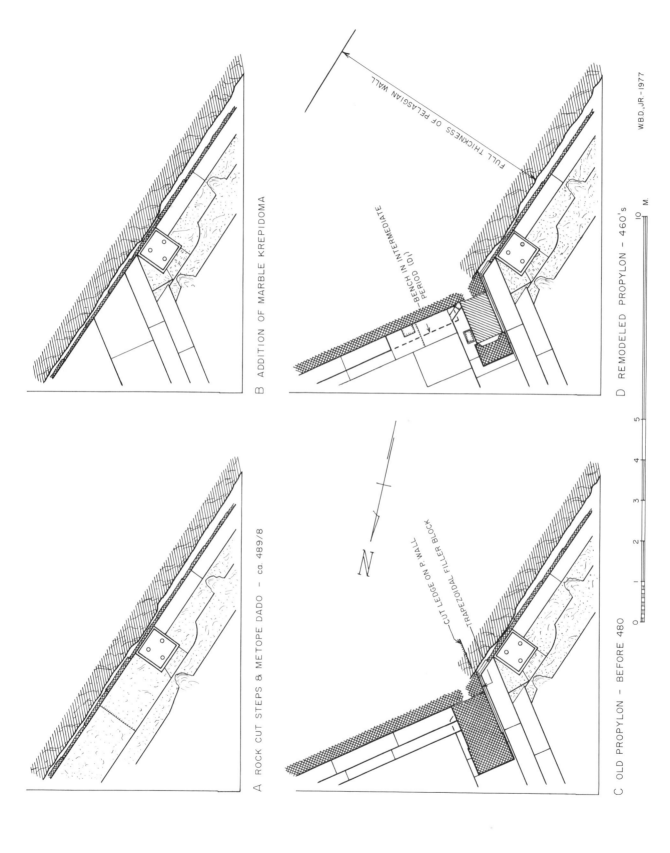

A ROCK CUT STEPS & METOPE DADO – ca. 489/8

B ADDITION OF MARBLE KREPIDOMA

C OLD PROPYLON – BEFORE 480

D REMODELED PROPYLON – 460's

CUT LEDGE ON P. WALL

TRAPEZOIDAL FILLER BLOCK

BENCH IN INTERMEDIATE PERIOD (D₁)

FULL THICKNESS OF PELASGIAN WALL

WBD,JR.-1977

Period plans of the forecourt and the Propylon in area II

PLATE 5

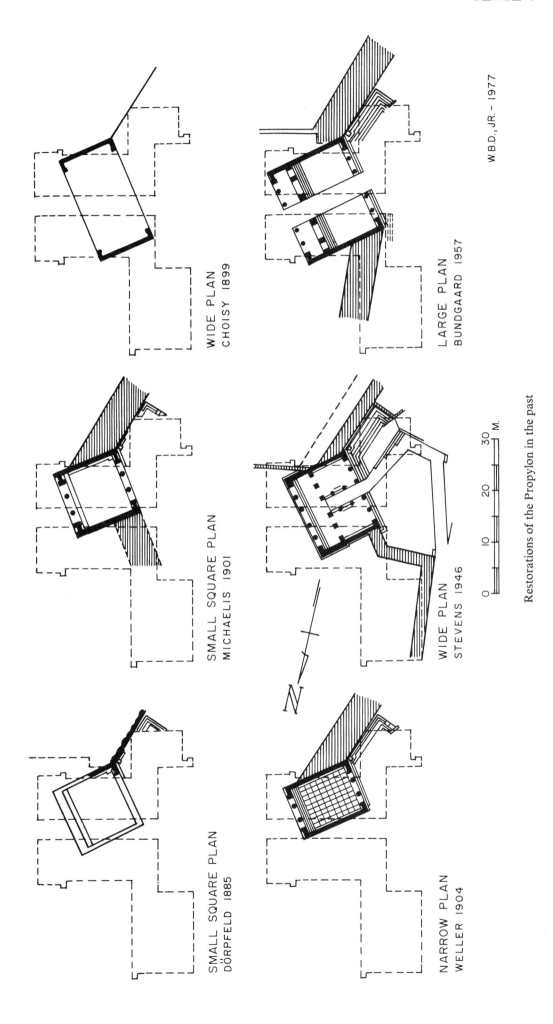

WIDE PLAN
CHOISY 1899

SMALL SQUARE PLAN
MICHAELIS 1901

SMALL SQUARE PLAN
DÖRPFELD 1885

LARGE PLAN
BUNDGAARD 1957

WIDE PLAN
STEVENS 1946

NARROW PLAN
WELLER 1904

W.B.D., JR. – 1977

Restorations of the Propylon in the past

30 M.

20

10

0

PLATE 6

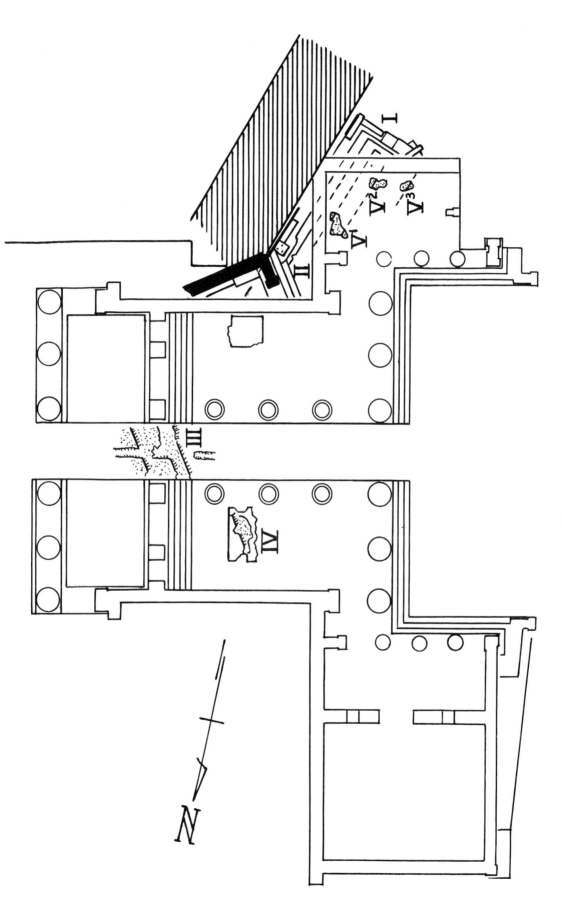

Location plan of areas I-V

PLATE 7

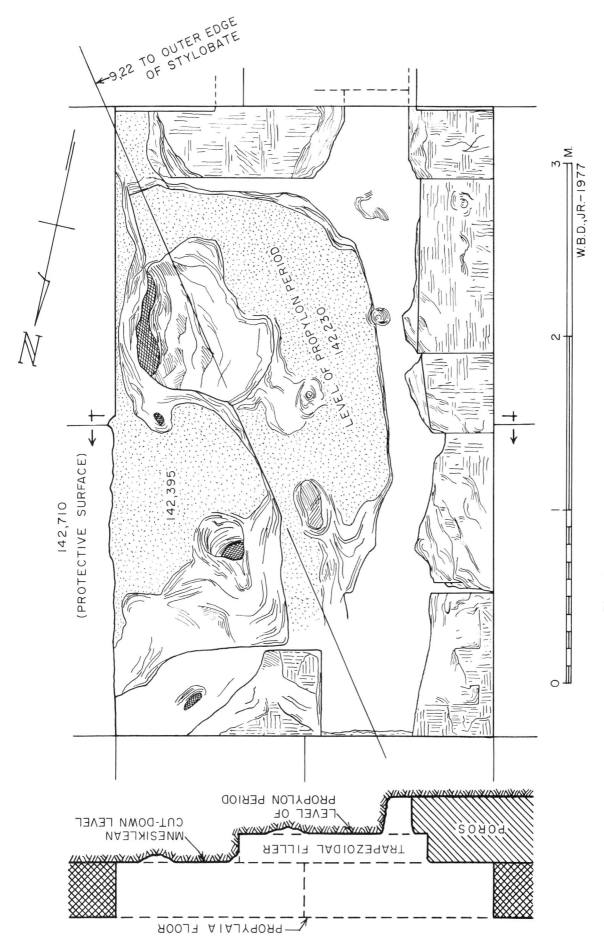

9.22 TO OUTER EDGE OF STYLOBATE

N

142,710
(PROTECTIVE SURFACE)

LEVEL OF PROPYLON PERIOD
142,230

142,395

LEVEL OF PROPYLON PERIOD

MNESIKLEAN CUT-DOWN LEVEL

TRAPEZOIDAL FILLER

POROS

PROPYLAIA FLOOR

W.B.D.,JR.-1977

0   1   2   3 M.

Plan of area IV in the north aisle of the Propylaia

PLATE 8

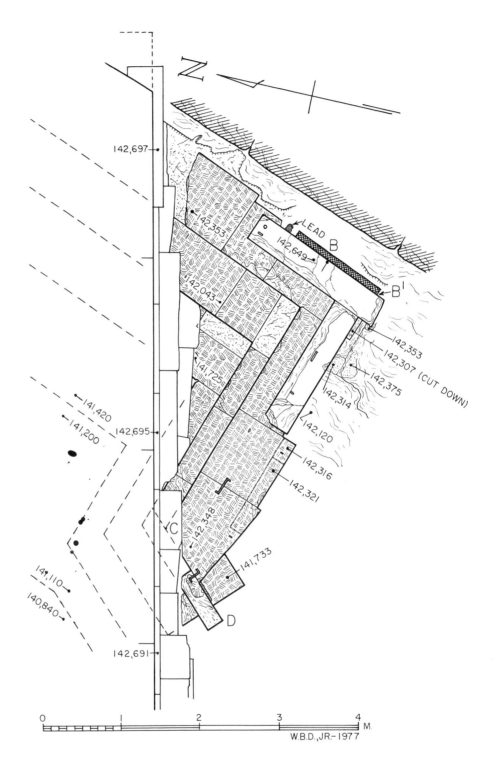

Actual state plan of area I

PLATE 9

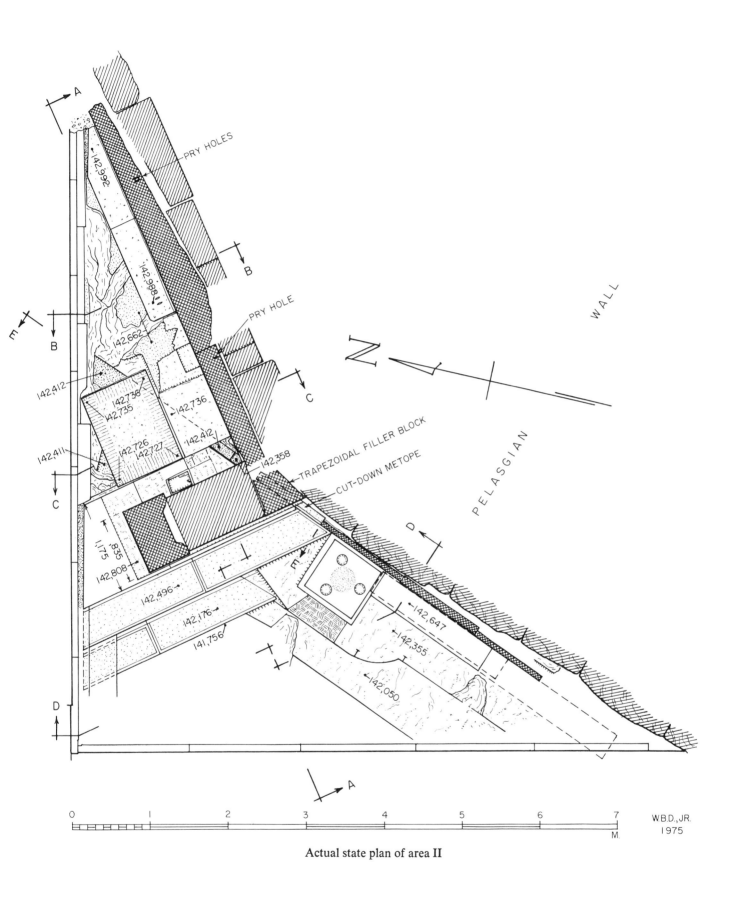

Actual state plan of area II

PLATE 10

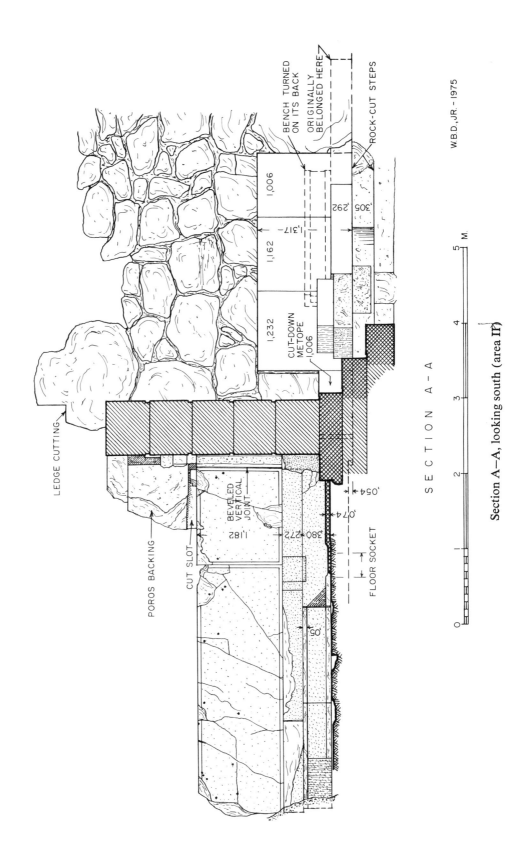

SECTION A–A

Section A–A, looking south (area II)

W.B.D., JR. - 1975

PLATE 11

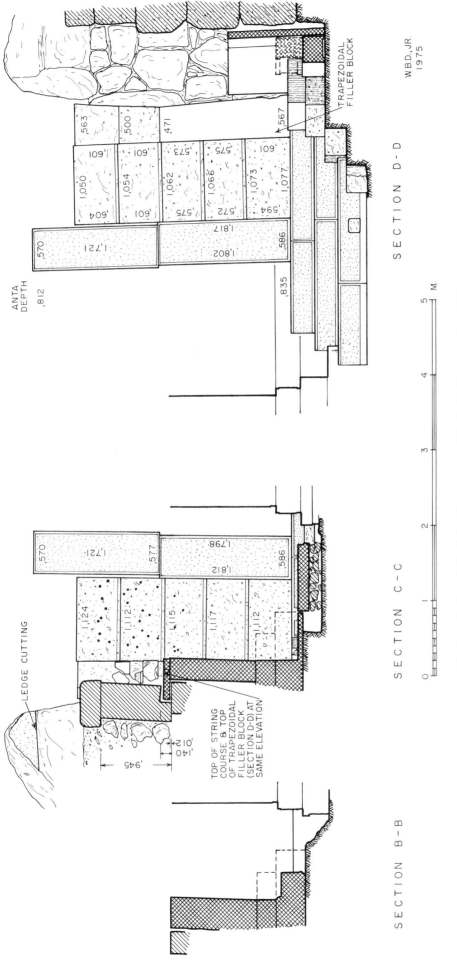

W.B.D., JR.
1975

SECTION B–B   SECTION C–C   SECTION D–D

Sections **B–B** and **C–C**, looking west, and **D–D**, looking east (area II)

PLATE 12

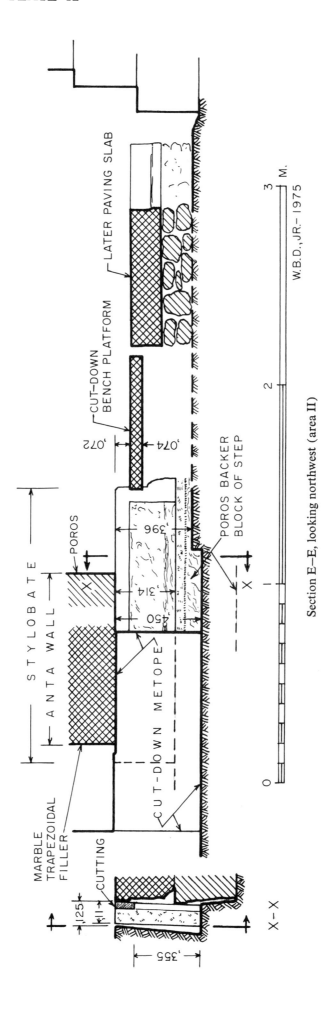

PLATE 12

LATER PAVING SLAB

CUT-DOWN BENCH PLATFORM

.072   .074

STYLOBATE

ANTA WALL

POROS

.396

.314

.450

POROS BACKER BLOCK OF STEP

CUT-DOWN METOPE

MARBLE TRAPEZOIDAL FILLER

CUTTING

.125

.355

X—X

Section E—E, looking northwest (area II)

W.B.D., JR.—1975

0   1   2   3   M.

PLATE 13

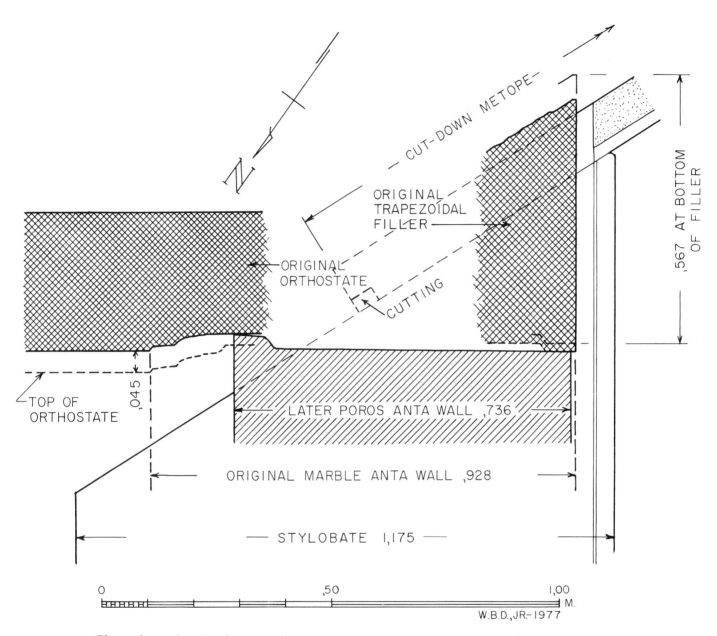

CUT-DOWN METOPE

ORIGINAL
TRAPEZOIDAL
FILLER

ORIGINAL
ORTHOSTATE

CUTTING

,567 AT BOTTOM
OF FILLER

TOP OF
ORTHOSTATE

,045

LATER POROS ANTA WALL ,736

ORIGINAL MARBLE ANTA WALL ,928

STYLOBATE 1,175

0   ,50   1,00
                                                  M.
                                        W.B.D., JR.- 1977

Plan at the south end of the anta wall (area II) at the level of the bottom of the orthostates

PLATE 14

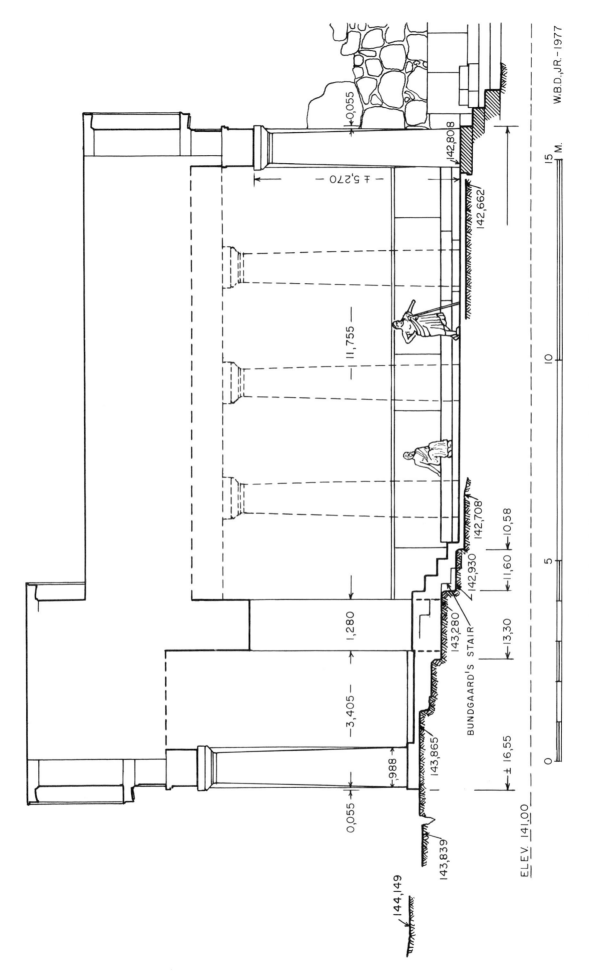

Restored section through the Propylon during the original period, looking south

PLATE 15

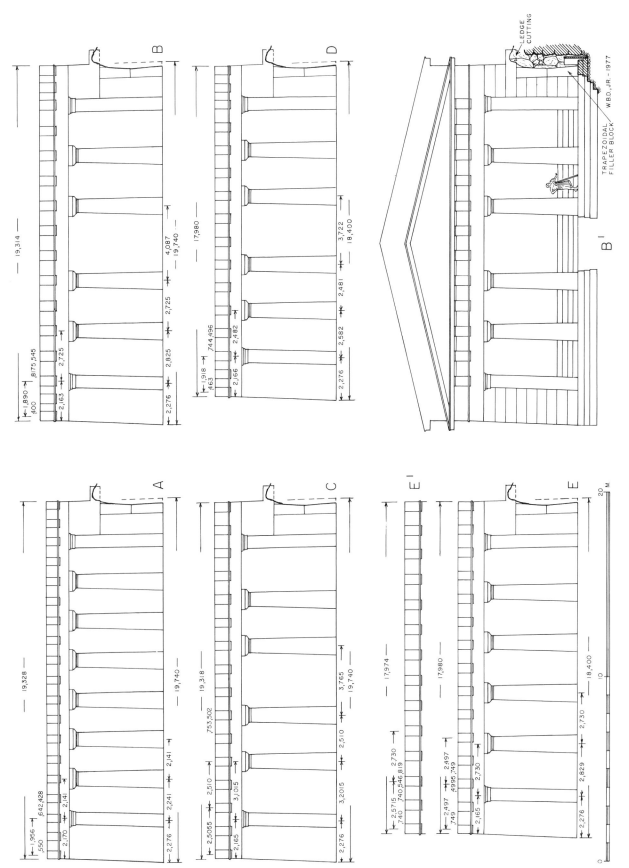

Schemes for the restored elevation of the west facade of the Propylon during the original period

PLATE 16

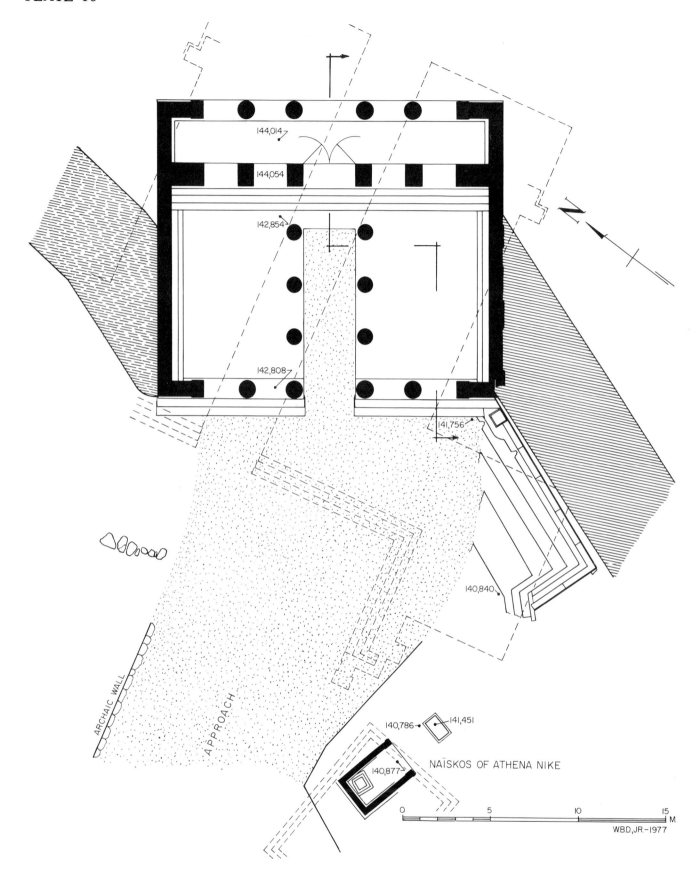

144,014

144,054

142,854

142,808

141,756

140,840

ARCHAIC WALL

APPROACH

140,786 → ☐ ← 141,451

NAÏSKOS OF ATHENA NIKE

140,877

0   5   10   15
|_____| M.

WBD, JR-1977

Restored plan of the Propylon during the original period

PLATE 17

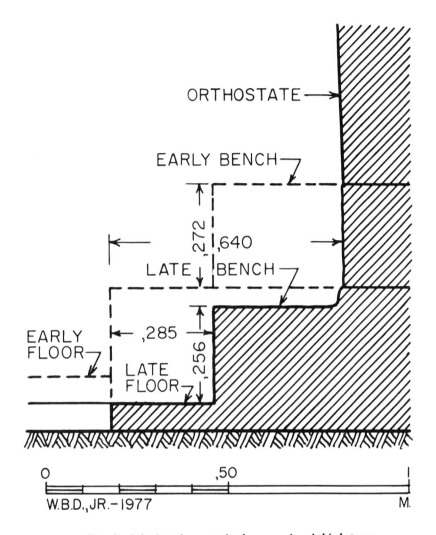

ORTHOSTATE

EARLY BENCH

,272

,640

LATE BENCH

EARLY
FLOOR

,285

,256

LATE
FLOOR

0   ,50

W.B.D.,JR.-1977   M.

Detail of the interior seats in the second and third stages

PLATE 18

a. Detail of cuttings in the southwest corner of the Propylon, looking southwest

b. Cut-down metope and bedrock behind the stylobate
1. Cut-down metope
2. Anathyrosis of stylobate
3. Filler slab to cover gap
   at end of stylobate
4. Poros anta wall

PLATE 19

a. Detail of cuttings in the southwest corner of the Propylon, looking southeast

b. Southwest corner inside the Propylon showing the rock-cut continuation for the metopes

PLATE 20

a. South flank wall of the Propylon

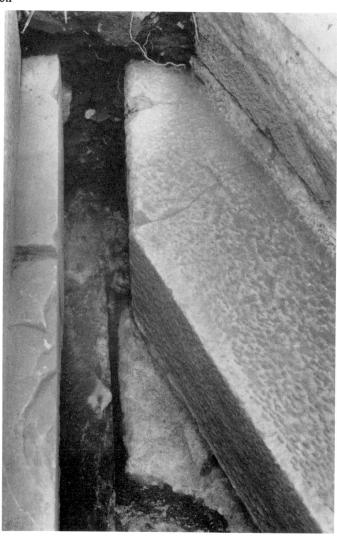

b. Mnesiklean chamfer of the wall bench in the Propylon, looking east

PLATE 21

b. Exterior of the Propylon showing the krepidoma (DAI Akr. 386)

a. Inner face of the parastas and the poros back-up of the south flank wall
(DAI Akr. 385)

PLATE 22

a. Stylobate and anta, looking east

b. Anta and anta wall, looking northeast

The paving blocks which now fill the forecourt were placed in the 1950's

PLATE 23

a. Forecourt, looking southeast

b. Cut-down metope outside the Propylon

PLATE 24

Forecourt and rock-cut steps, looking southeast (DAI Akr. 387)

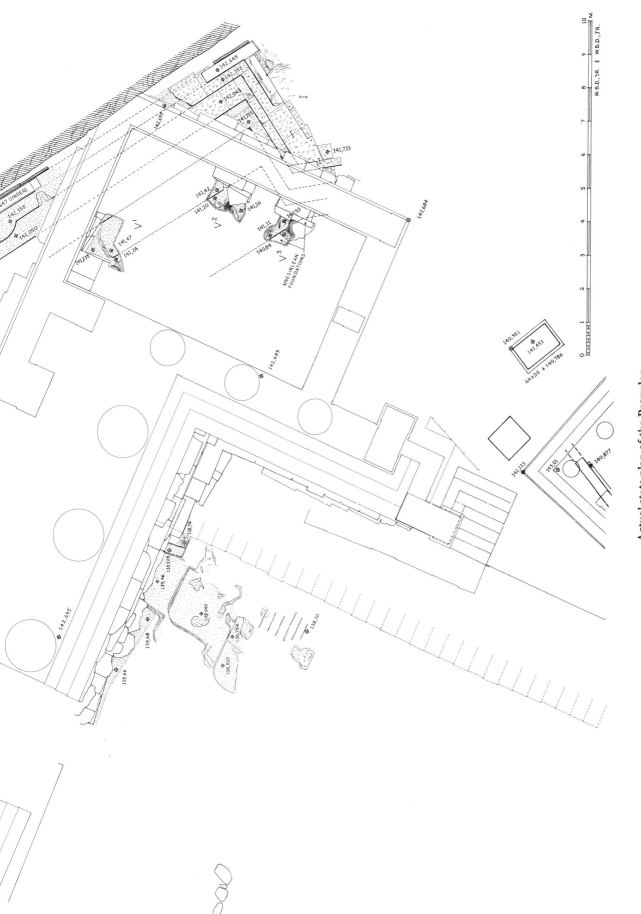

Actual state plan of the Propylon

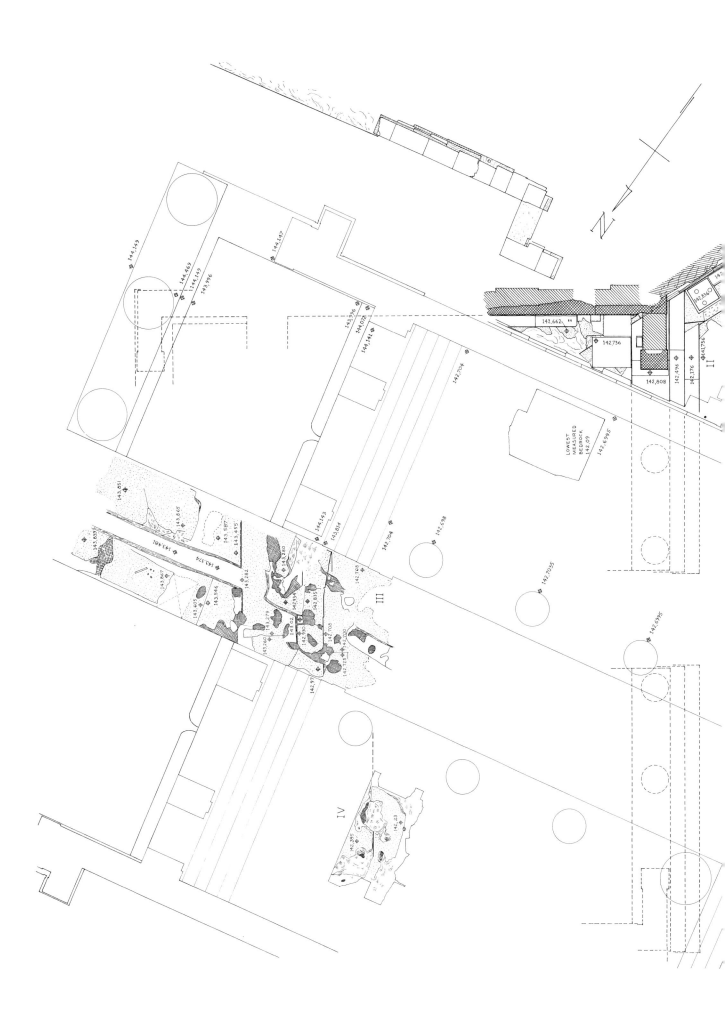

144.149
144.469
144.149
143.996
144.147
143.996
144.072
144.141

142.662
142.736
142.808
142.856
142.496
142.176
141.756
II

142.704
LOWEST
MEASURED
BEDROCK
142.09
142.6995

143.651
143.865
143.587
143.455
144.143
143.814
142.704
142.698
143.635
143.481
143.374
143.280
143.867
143.282
142.704
III
142.708
142.934
143.546
142.835
142.7035
143.605
143.279
143.62
142.390
142.606
142.740
142.725 142.97
143.260
142.6995

IV
142.23
142.395